Spoken into the Void:
Collected Essays 1897–1900

OPPOSITIONS BOOKS

Introduction by Aldo Rossi
Translation by Jane O. Newman
and John H. Smith

Adolf Loos

Spoken into the Void

Collected Essays 1897-1900

Published for the Graham Foundation for Advanced Studies
in the Fine Arts, Chicago, Illinois, and
The Institute for Architecture and Urban Studies,
New York, New York, by

The MIT Press
Cambridge, Massachusetts, and London, England

1982

Copyright © 1982 by
The Institute for Architecture and
Urban Studies and
The Massachusetts Institute of
Technology

Third printing, 1989

First MIT Press paperback edition, 1987

*Library of Congress Cataloguing in
Publication Data*
Loos, Adolf, 1870–1933.
Spoken into the void.
(Oppositions Books)
Translation of: Ins Leere gesprochen,
1897–1900.
"Published for the Graham
Foundation for Advanced Studies in
the Fine Arts, Chicago, Illinois, and
the Institute for Architecture and
Urban Studies, New York,
New York."
Includes index.
1. Art industries and trade—
History—19th century—Addresses,
essays, lectures.
I. Title.
II. Series.
NK775.L6313 1982 670 82-10100
ISBN 0-262-12097-6 (hard)
        0-262-62057-X (paper)

Typography by The Old Typosopher in
Century Expanded. Printed and bound by
Halliday Lithograph Corporation in the
United States of America.

*Cover drawing of Adolf Loos by Oskar
Kokoschka, 1916.*

OPPOSITIONS BOOKS

Editors
Peter Eisenman
Kenneth Frampton

Executive Editor
Joan Ockman

Assistant Editor
Thomas Mellins

Editorial Intern
Andrew Cohen

Design
Massimo Vignelli

Design Coordinator
Abigail Sturges

Production
Heidi King

Photography
Mary Bachmann

Contents

Editor's Note

This translation of Ins Leere gesprochen *by Adolf Loos is based on the 1932 edition published by Brenner Verlag in Austria. It differs in several respects from the first edition published by Georges Crès & Cie. in France in 1921. Besides excising a number of specific references to people and places as well as carefully reworking his language throughout, Loos added the essay "Potemkin City" to the later edition and removed two essays, perhaps for reasons of redundancy. We have included these two essays as an appendix here, along with the foreword to the first edition, in which Loos recounts the history of his difficulties in having the book published in Austria.*

The title, which we have rendered as Spoken into the Void, *is somewhat more colloquial in the original. An alternative translation might be "falling upon deaf ears." It should also be noted that in the German version the non-proper nouns are not capitalized, a typographic idiosyncrasy that would have been immediately apparent to the German reader. Loos specifically explains the reasons for his breach of convention in the Foreword, although he (or his typographer) is not entirely consistent about implementing it. We have tried to follow suit wherever German nouns have been retained in the translated text, but have chosen to use the conventional style elsewhere in order to avoid awkwardness.*

Most of the essays in the book were initially published in newspapers of the day as reviews of exhibitions then taking place in Vienna. Those published in the liberal Neue Freie Presse *were written on the occasion of the Vienna Jubilee Exhibition of 1898. This was a six-month-long fair celebrating the fiftieth anniversary of Emperor Franz Joseph's accession to the Austrian throne. The events took place in and around the Rotunda, an exhibition pavilion in the Prater built for the Vienna World's Fair of 1873. In an article of 1898 in* Die Wage, *Karl Kraus described the purpose of the Jubilee as "to make foreign countries aware of the high level of our productive capacity in the crafts and of our strides in the second half of the century" and at the same time to allow the Viennese themselves to appreciate "what we have paid too little attention to in the last fifty years."*

With two exceptions, the essays originally appeared unillustrated. For the present volume, we have provided a visual text that is intended to parallel the written one. These images, most of them culled from contemporary periodicals, newspapers, and books, illustrate some of the objects that Loos discusses; others relate more broadly to the cultural context as a whole. Without overwhelming the essays themselves, we have tried to illuminate verbal description with visual references, and above all to bring to life the Viennese ambience of abendländische Kultur *at the moment that Loos was writing in and about it. (In the two instances where illustrations did appear with the original articles, we have included examples of them.) Editor's footnotes at the end of the book are also intended to shed light on a few obscurities.*

Much of the pictorial research for this book was carried out at the New York Public Library, the Austrian Institute, the Avery Library of Columbia University, and the library of the Metropolitan Museum of Art. We wish particularly to thank Mr. Walter Zervas of the New York Public Library for his cooperation with the project and for making the library's collection so accessible to us. We have drawn on the following collections of the New York Public Library, Astor, Lenox and Tilden Foundations: the Arts, Prints and Photographs Division; the Science and Technology Research Center; and the

General Research Division. We are also grateful to Ms. Frederike Zeitlhofer of the Austrian Institute for her assistance with a number of technical matters in the translation.

Kurt Forster made several helpful suggestions relative to the translation in the early stages. The majority of the photographs were taken by Mary Bachmann. Tom Mellins and Andrew Cohen devoted long hours and much ingenuity to the pictorial research. Finally, a word of thanks to Daniel Shapiro for his excellent job of typesetting and to Christopher Sweet for his skillful proofreading.

J. O.

Introduction

Adolf Loos's writings are an integral part of his life's work; together with his designs, his constructions, and his biography, they display a coherence rarely found in an artist of the modern era. The totality of his writings, which arise from a great variety of circumstances and are often fragmentary, nevertheless presents this almost systematic coherence, as though it were really a treatise on architecture that he was writing. Without doubt his work is full of references to the Vienna of his day, a vastly rich culture in its wider European context, but we would probably do well not to insist too much on this aspect.

Nor is there any doubt of Loos's references to Karl Kraus, who, along with Peter Altenberg, was one of his best friends; or of his affinities to Robert Musil, despite the vastly different personalities of the two men. The aphorisms of Kraus reappear in Loos's prose in plain view, saving us the trouble of vainly researching the borrowings and the original concepts; Musil's "man without qualities" at times actually seems to be a physical profile of Loos, not to mention an intellectual one. And we should try to learn more about Loos's other relations, some of which are perhaps purely a matter of poetic intuition, such as those with Georg Trakl, who increasingly is emerging as the greatest modern poet in the German language and who came to dedicate two poems to Loos. Beyond this, despite the importance of the cultural circles in which Loos moved, this game of referencing appears to be a rather esoteric one; in a publication celebrating Loos's sixtieth birthday, several testimonials, especially those of Le Corbusier, Walter Gropius, and Bruno Taut, are thoroughly incomprehensible. As Edoardo Persico correctly noted, "He [Loos] was often mistakenly quoted in many matters and his assertions, taken out of context, were used to defend positions that he did not in fact support."

It is apparent that he was already a legend by his sixtieth year, the date of this singular "Homage to Adolf Loos." For modern architecture he was a figure whom it was impolitic to attack, and at the same time one who was too important not to be assimilated in some way. A similar fate was experienced by Heinrich Tessenow, whom not even the harshest modernist accusation, that of being branded a Fascist, could succeed in effacing. But while Tessenow kept himself apart by confining himself to the integrity of architecture and its craft—an integrity thinly veiled by irony—Loos possessed an unusual ability that perhaps he himself did not fully understand: a peculiar power to irritate, or even better, to unsettle the public.

This inevitably meant his ostracism as a man, and more precisely as a worker, at the same time that he was being accepted as a legend. The ancient Greeks knew that a man's character was his fate; such was Loos's fate as well.

The power to irritate is closely related to the ability to amuse oneself, and the reader who is not overly confused by the academic pedantry will amuse himself greatly with a good deal of the writings collected here. Certain pieces, written in the "journalistic" manner, have provoked me to laughter and remind me of another artist who loved to confront problems with a sense of humor, namely James Joyce. There is no doubt that these contemporaries of Freud were well aware that "every joke is a murder," and may be placed among those artists whom Manfredo Tafuri defines as "villainous." But Loos, apart from being "villainous" in a higher sense, is often "impudent" in the usual sense of the word. While preaching the uselessness of furnishings provided by architects and at the same time of the do-it-yourself method—and from this we should logically deduce that one style is as good as another—he considers Secession furniture actually to be criminal: "The day will come," he writes, "when the furnishing of a prison cell by the court decorator Schulz or by Professor Van de Velde will be considered to be an aggravation of the penalty." This is a statement which, deprived of its sarcasm, could be said to contain a moralism much like that of Gropius. In speaking of his mythic America, the significance of which we shall see more clearly below, Loos seems to be delighted with a meal whose main dish is oatmeal; elsewhere he notes the fine eating habits of his much-maligned countrymen, "for the Austrians know a lot about good cooking." This unexplained assertion is equivalent to another on German cuisine: "The German people eat what they are served; they are always satisfied, pay the bill, and leave."

Throughout Loos's writings one can find many quotations of this sort, some even more amusing and sarcastic than the above, and all of them supported by a rigorous sense of logic, a persistent sense of involvement, and an anger akin to disillusionment. This feeling of disillusionment is much broader than any sort of disappointment with society or personal matters; it is centered on an abstract idea, a battle in which the enemy is a priori elusive, ungraspable, and not unlike the enemy of the mystic—sin. In this case the enemy is stupidity and lack of understanding and a sense of the end of things. Speaking of Karl Kraus, Loos summed up his friend's thought and anxiety, saying, "He fears the end of the world." The end of the world here is also the end of a world without meaning, where the search for authentic quality involves a man without specific qualities, where the great architecture of immutable meanings carries with it a sort of paralysis of creativity and the non-recognition of any progress of reason. Truth, architecture, art, the ancients—all this is behind Adolf Loos who, like all men of this kind, was well aware that he was traveling down a road without hope.

This attitude also calls into question the meaning of trade, of day-to-day labor, and, consequently, of how one earns a living. On the one hand are the static architecture of monuments, the great architecture of the ancients, and the rather complicated possibility of "becoming" an architect; on the other hand are the minor activities whose efficacy he denies, such as the ordering of a house, its furnishing, its interior design. Loos does not hide this contradiction—on the contrary, he posits it as part of his working terminology, and in one of his responses to a reader of *Das Andere* he actually affirms that he will continue to furnish stores, cafes, and private homes, even though such activity is not by any means architectural—especially in an era when "every carpet designer defines himself as an architect." And why does he do all this? Because this trade gives him something to live on, and because he can do it well: "Just like in America where I earned my living for a while by washing dishes. But one could support oneself just as easily doing something else too." The contradiction between art and trade is so played down that the argument touches on an aspect that the idealist point of view has always neglected, that of the artist's means of subsistence. As always, Loos condemns the moralism of action by taking a position that is directly opposed to the economic romanticism of the Modern Movement. Each person will live in his own house, according to his own personality, but in all probability someone will ask for advice about this or that problem, or more simply will have better things to do than to furnish his own house; then the architect, trying to do his job well, will advise him. That is all. In this light Loos's sarcasm directed against the Secession is easier to understand; what Loos is really attacking in his contemporaries is not so much their style or their taste (even though he finds it abominable)—what he cannot tolerate is the "redemptive" value that they assign to their own actions. One trade is as good as another; and even a trade like washing dishes can be done well provided one breaks as few as possible.

This certainly is one aspect which "modern architecture," so committed to mythifying its relations with industry and reformist politics, has been unable to admit and unwilling to discuss. Modern architects have always tried to assign this moralistic or "redemptive" value to what they have done, with the exception of a few such as Tessenow and certainly Mies van der Rohe. Mies is well aware of the problem of "style," and his attitude toward tradition is very similar to that of Loos; behind his work stand Schinkel and German classicism, the purity of white marble, and the profile of the tympanum, all of which he seeks out and rediscovers. The skyscrapers of Chicago were conceived as, and still are, urban towers unconcerned with any false social problematics. They are beautiful buildings, more difficult to imitate and assimilate than is commonly believed. Le Corbusier's Marseille housing block, when seen today in the midst of the sea of buildings surrounding it, actually seems ridiculous if one considers the social purposes it once claimed to fulfill.

The writings and the work of Loos possess such a sense of completeness that considerations of this sort reappear in all of his writings and on occasions of the most varied sort. In "How the State Takes Care of Us," this dandy who at times seems so detached from society puts forth a precise and demystifying denunciation of reformist "good will"; in denouncing the shameful condition of children forced to live by their wits in the streets, he does not launch his attack against the situation itself, but against the state which does not want to see this problem as part of its so-called protection of the family. After a brief description of a poor Viennese family, Loos writes vitriolically, "There are no dangers of the streets. . . . *There is only a danger of the family.* . . . Doctors claim that syphilis is not nearly as dangerous in childhood as in adulthood. And psychologists claim that masturbation in pairs is not nearly as harmful to the character as masturbating alone. It almost makes me believe the masses are better off in any case." Forget the reformism of *Existenzminimum* and the much-vaunted social values of the modern *Siedlung;* here one seems to be reading the young Lenin of the attacks against economic romanticism.

And architecture itself? Architecture is still the central theme of Loos's thought, and among his essays is a piece on the competition sponsored by the *Chicago Tribune,* a piece which, like the one on the Michaelerhaus and "Ornament and Crime," is essential to an understanding of the meaning of architecture.

This latter piece is to my mind particularly pertinent today, at a time when "postmodernism" is being praised with the same superficiality and the same arguments as modernism was: with everything packaged into a discussion of forms—forms which "change as quickly as a lady's hats." For Loos the experience with the *Chicago Tribune* competition is a decisive one. In this experience he measures himself against the classical world, the great architectural works, and the American city, which made such a deep impression on him. It is certain that Loos is one of the very few architects who understood American architecture (this was also the case later with certain Soviet architects); what particularly impressed him were certainly New York and perhaps St. Louis, and to a lesser extent Chicago. While European modernists were getting excited about the constructions of Wright, dreaming about who knows what sort of exotic democracy, Loos was resolutely exploring the streets of downtown New York, amazed at the dark, immense buildings of Broadway and the perspectives offered by the buildings of Wall Street. The beauty of this nucleus of American business struck him in much the same way that the beauty of aristocratic and capitalist London had once struck Engels. The Austrian master understood that this was the form of the architecture with which one had to come to terms; as in ancient Rome, Venice, or Paris, the architecture of the city was a totality of exchanges, interrelationships, similitudes, and grafts. And from all this a new architecture would be born; the classical orders would be used according to the specifications of the theoreticians or altogether overturned; green Corinthian capitals would enclose large window frames made of iron; each fragile "collage" would vanish in the strength of the materials used; the spires at the top of the skyscrapers would always be different. Loos was to write that "the architect is a bricklayer who has studied Latin"; I remember that for Ernesto Rogers this was the best definition of the architect that he had ever heard, and I would tend to agree with him. Thus, Loos's passion for architecture is manifest only when he is confronted by mastery in construction, great Roman architecture, Fischer von Erlach, eighteenth-century building, and the masters who transcended construction itself and remain as fixed points of reference in the history of civilization. As in the writings of Baudelaire, the influence of invention on life is marked by fixed reference points, points which enable one to grasp fully the changes of life itself, in the same way that the fixity of lighthouses enables ships to navigate. The notion of the bricklayer who has studied Latin calls to mind Palladio, who did not finish his designs so that he could translate classical texts; it calls to mind Leonardo and Petrarch who in their old age studied Greek that they might better understand the ancients.

In his emphasis on monuments and antiquity, Loos is nevertheless perhaps the first to speak of tradition in a modern sense; and he speaks of it as a man of the city, one who knows its places and houses as if they were family photographs, one who loves old things and their ruin, who knows how each place is steeped in personal history and sees with sadness how all of this is destined to perish. With regard to the harsh criticisms directed at his Michaelerhaus he writes, ". . . Any word that I happen to read praising our old city or attempting to save our disappearing cityscape provokes a stronger response in me than in most others. . . . I have always entertained the illusion of resolving [problems] like our old Viennese masters. . . ." The old Viennese masters are the saddler and the shoemaker, the artisans about whom he writes in his articles: people with whom he tarries a bit and from whom he learns; and at the same time they are the great masters, like Fischer von Erlach. There is something both affectionate and restrictive in his phrase "the old masters"; they are not the *ancients*, and they are probably people who have not "studied Latin." The distinction between architecture and city planning, an abstract separation, becomes concrete fact and the only real choice that the modern city has to make. The difference between Loos and the "modernist" architects is so profound that there is no communication between them; it is not a question of decoration or function, of the classical style or the new styles, but of the defense of the city of man against any utopia that is a slave to power. Only today are we fully able to understand these words, having seen cities and countrysides destroyed by the "system" and by modern architecture's complaisant victory. But modern architecture is an architecture already grown old, beginning with the districts of Frankfurt and any *ville radieuse*; its polemic has by now almost faded away in the wreckage of its own destruction. Meanwhile others, using similar arguments, are now trying to turn the old city or its few remaining fragments into a museum. Not even Loos himself would today know where to stand among leftist demagogy, political intrigue, and the ruthless power governing our cities. In light of what we know now, the targets of Loos's attacks seem almost naive and undeserving; the academic world, the Secession, Professor Van de Velde, German functionalism, and other such ghosts appear perhaps to have been only stupid and innocent pawns.

It would be like writing the history of the "urban development plans" (a sinister phrase that the young have already forgotten) for the cities of Western Europe; but frankly, who would want to?

At the start of this essay I spoke of a "mythic America" which appears in the writings of Loos. It is a theme essential to an understanding of the Viennese master's polemics and point of view. Clearly this conception does not refer to that architecture whose influences and impressions are direct and explicit; it refers instead to a positive world, to an example of an almost perfect society. To the reader of today, and probably to Loos's contemporaries, this idea seems almost ridiculous (and it is upon first reading).

But what was the "America" theme for Loos? Actually it was the opposition between a direct, brutal world and the hypocrisy of the European, and especially Austrian, system. As we have seen, Loos liked to take extreme positions, and his every extreme verges on the irrational; but undoubtedly his attraction to America, and more generally to Anglo-Saxon culture, was the result of his choice of a generic type that stood for progress, as was also the case, conversely, in his sarcasm toward all that was German.

Reading Loos, I have always thought that his "America" was not much different from the America of the Italian anti-Fascists, of Cesare Pavese and Elio Vittorini in particular. In the 1950s these two great Italian writers used America as material for invention, as a pretext not only for their interpretation of texts they translated, but also for their own novels. In film there is also Luchino Visconti, who begins his discovery of Italy with an American romance; and this blending of a foreign world of aimless vagabonds and great open spaces with the equally aimless world of the Po Valley lost within the national equilibrium is the plot and landscape of his *Obsession*. This liberty, which fascinated Europeans because of its anomaly, because its roots were European, is also in fact the key to reading Vittorini's "American" anthology, as that author himself made clear by placing at the beginning of the book the following passage by D. H. Lawrence: ". . . Let us then ask ourselves again, why did they escape to America? For a lot of reasons. But least of all because they desired any sort of liberty, any positive liberty. Actually they needed to get away. A simple enough reason. To get away. Away from what? All things considered, to get away from themselves, to escape themselves. To escape anything . . ."

When in the introduction to the Italian translation of Loos's writings Joseph Rykwert writes that "excluding the visits to his cousins in Philadelphia, it seems that his stay in America was spent in restaurant kitchens, washing dishes at night, in YMCA rooms, in miserable lodgings, and occasionally writing a bit of journalism to earn his keep . . . ," he makes a correct statement as far as we can tell, but one to which he has not given much thought. In my opinion, the Loos of this period (leaving aside the almost irritating aspect of the dandy who mentions repeatedly, *ad nauseam*, his apprenticeship as a dishwasher) is quite conscious of that America of "escape" emphasized by Vittorini, and in a way he seems to prefigure the "on the road" sensibility that was later to find its poets. Such would be another ingenious show of intuition on the part of Loos, even if it remains but the speculation of a critic. Actually, in Loos's entire body of work there is always the desire to attack institutions and to reject a "positive liberty." Liberty seems to be something forbidden. It belongs to the Papuan native who can decorate himself as he pleases; it belongs to the tomb; it belongs to the Doric column, which can only be copied.

As in Georg Trakl—and the parallel is a relevant and affectionate one—only in the singular testimony of permanence is there progress. In his last years Loos writes, as though in an obituary, "We know that all the artistic fuss over styles of living—in any country—do not make the dog move away from the warmth of the stove, and that all the traffic of associations, school professorships, periodicals, exhibitions, and so on has not produced anything new; all evolution in modern craftsmanship (excluding the influence of new discoveries) is in the vision of two eyes. And these eyes are my own. And this means that nobody has understood anything. But I am not waiting for my obituary. I am writing it now, myself."

Perhaps the "villainous" artist here is abandoning thought in order to unveil his own passion; even his harsh polemic against his contemporaries fades into the distance. All that remains is the tattooed body of the Papuan and the dog that will not move away from the warmth of the stove. Architecture is here identified with the body of man and animal.

I have already mentioned that the *Chicago Tribune* competition was decisive for Loos. In this experience he seems to have confronted both the themes of what he calls "the great architecture" and his own contradictions. But the artist's contradictions fade in his rejection of originality; to Loos's mind, only unimportant artists are original, and we should willingly concede to them the right to begin *ex nihilo*. Thus he writes: "For my project I have chosen the column as a model. . . . I fear that the strongest objections will concern the ugliness of my building. . . . No elaborate diagram is capable of describing the effect of these columns; the smooth, polished surfaces of the cube and the fluting of the columns will unsettle the observer. It will be a surprise, and will cause a big stir for these times. . . . The great Doric column will one day be built. If not in Chicago, then in another city. If not for the *Chicago Tribune*, then for some other newspaper. If not by me, then by another architect."

In spite of this prophecy, the great Doric column will probably never be built; but with this timeless, hallucinatory image in words, the Viennese master has left behind him the world of the polemics of the Moderns and the purity of materials, of industrial design and all the nonsense of the furniture architects or of the decorators who call themselves architects.

And with regard to the image of the Doric column, it would be useless to make any comment, presentation, or introduction, or to engage in the kind of idle prattle that makes up a good deal of the traffic of associations, school professorships, periodicals, and exhibitions. It is certain that this traffic will continue forever, but it is also certain that someone will always be around to expose its stupidity. Loos's great Doric column places him, however tumultuously, among the great masters, for we can see that there is a great difference between speaking about the Greeks and speaking as a Greek. Thus, while lesser artists will seek their own original terrain, the best will choose to imitate the ancients and speak like them once again.

This is the best lesson I have learned from Adolf Loos.

Aldo Rossi
Translated by Stephen Sartarelli

Foreword

This book contains the essays I wrote up to and during the year 1900. They were written at a time when I had a thousand things to think about. For didactic reasons I had to express my true opinions in sentences that years later still cause me to shudder as I read them. Only at the insistence of my students have I in time come to agree to the publication of these essays.

The architect Heinrich Kulka, one of my loyal students, prepared the first edition; it was issued by the publishing house of Georges Crès and Co. in Paris, since no German publishing house dared to take it on in 1920. It was probably the only book in the last hundred years which was originally written in German, but which was published in France.

In this second edition, the essays have been reworked in both style and content, but I have maintained their original tone. I have made one small addition in the form of the essay "The Potemkin City."

It will probably annoy the reader that the nouns are printed with lower-case initials.[1] Jacob Grimm[2] has already demonstrated that this method of writing is the logical consequence of using Roman type; his students (that is, all subsequent Germanists) have since printed only in this fashion.

I insert here a few sentences by Jacob Grimm from the foreword to his German dictionary:
"All writing was originally done in capital letters, after the manner in which they were carved into stone. For swift writing on papyrus and parchment, the letters were reduced in size and connected; the characteristics of the small letters were more or less modified as a result. The distorted and deformed shape of the capital letters developed out of the initials in manuscripts, which were painted in with a brush. . . . In Latin books, proper names as well as initials were emphasized by the use of capital letters. This is still done today as an aid to the reader. In the course of the sixteenth century, the abuse occurred, at first tentatively and then in the end decisively, of expanding this emphasis to include each and every noun. As a result, the earlier advantage was lost. Proper names became indistinguishable from the masses of nouns. Writing overall began to acquire a colorful but awkward appearance, since the capital letters took up two to three times the space of the small letters. Conciseness and facility of expression, which were never a German speaker's strong point, retreated entirely before these clumsy and pompous letters. In my view there is no doubt of the essential connection between this distorted fashion of writing [Fraktur[3]] and the purposeless proliferation of capital letters. The writer sought a presumed embellishment in these letters and *took pleasure in the writing of them because of both the flourishes and their multiplication. . . .*
Once a whole generation has adopted the new way of writing, not a single voice will be raised among those that follow in defense of the old. . . . If we have rid our houses of their gables and their projecting rafters, and have removed the powder from our hair, why should we retain such rubbish in our writing?"

I am convinced that Jacob Grimm's thinking will soon be taken up by all Germans. Besides having a German god, we also have a German script. And both are false. In the same passage Jacob Grimm says, "It is unfortunate that this tasteless and depraved script [Fraktur] is identified as 'German,' as if every fashionable abuse of ours ought to be stamped innately 'German' and thereby commended."

All of these sacred artifacts of "Germanness" are derived from something foreign and only became German because they were struck with paralysis while on German territory and could no longer change. They should all be thrown out with the rubbish. As a German, I wish to lodge a complaint against everything that has been abandoned by other peoples only to be proclaimed thereafter as German. I object to the barrier that is drawn again and again between that which is German and that which is human.

The rigid clinging to the practice of capitalizing nouns has as its consequence the return of language to a barbaric state. This derives from the abyss that opens up in the German mind between the written and the spoken word. It is impossible to utter a capital letter. Every one of us speaks without ever thinking of capital letters. But when the German takes pen in hand, he can no longer write as he thinks, as he speaks. The writer is unable to speak; the speaker cannot write. And in the end, the German can do neither.

Vienna, August 1921
Paris, July 1931

Adolf Loos

Essays on the Occasion of the Vienna Jubilee Exhibition of 1898

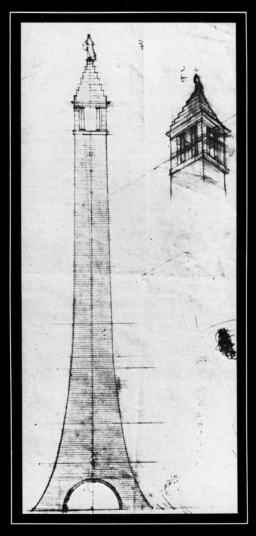

2 Project for the Emperor's Jubilee Memorial Church, Vienna. Adolf Loos, 1899.

When we stick close to our own turf, we never become aware of the treasures hidden at home. That which is first-rate is gradually taken for granted. But when we have taken a look around us, outside of us, then a sudden change occurs in our estimation of our homespun products.

I left home years ago[1] to acquaint myself with the architecture and industry on the other side of the Atlantic Ocean. At the time I was still totally convinced of the superiority of German crafts and handiwork. With pride and enthusiasm, I went through the German and Austrian sections in Chicago. I glanced with a sympathetic smile at the budding American "arts and crafts movement." But how that has all changed! My years of residence over there have had the effect that I still today blush with embarrassment when I think of the disgraceful representation of the German crafts in Chicago. These proud and splendid pieces of workmanship, these stylish display pieces—they were nothing more than philistine sham.

There were, however, two crafts that saved our prestige. Our Austrian prestige, that is, not the German, for here as well the Germans had nothing good to show for themselves. These crafts were the production of leather fancy-goods and the gold- and silversmith trades. They did not operate in the same way. While the producers of the former items were inclined to perform honestly in every line of work, one encountered some of the latter trade's products in the camp of the shams.

At the time I harbored a silent rage about these objects. There were wallets, cigar and cigarette cases, picture frames, writing implements, suitcases, bags, riding whips, canes, silver handles, water bottles, everything—all of it—smooth and polished, no ornament, no decoration. The silver was, at the very most, fluted or hammered. I was ashamed of these pieces. This was not the work of the arts and crafts! This was fashion! Fashion! What an appalling word! The greatest insult to the true and proper craftsman, which I still was at the time.

Of course, the Viennese bought such things gladly. They were called "tasteful," the efforts of the School of Applied Arts notwithstanding. In vain were the most beautiful objects of earlier periods displayed and their production encouraged. In the end, the gold- and silversmiths did as they were told. They even had their sketches made by the most famous men. But the objects thus produced just would not sell. The Viennese were incorrigible. (Of course, it was different in Germany. There the wallets and cigarette cases were overloaded with the loveliest Rococo ornamentation and found a great market. "Stylish" was the ticket.) The Viennese individual was persuaded only with great difficulty to submit his home furnishings to the new regime. But in matters of useful objects or of his own body he followed his own taste exclusively, and here he considered all ornament to be vulgar.

At any rate, I was still of a different mind at the time. But I do not hesitate to make it clear now that at that time even the silliest fop could have surpassed me in matters of taste. The strong wind of America and England has since stripped me of all prejudices against the products of my own time. Totally unprincipled men have attempted to spoil this time for us. We were always supposed to look back; we were always supposed to take another age as our model. But all of this has now retreated from me like a bad dream. Yes, our time is beautiful, so beautiful that I could not see living in any other. Our age is beautiful to look at, so beautiful that, had I the choice of picking out the garment of any other time at all,

3 View of the World's Columbian Exposition, Chicago, 1893. Loos visited the Chicago exhibition in 1893.

*4 Exhibition of German silver crafts
in the Manufacturers' Building,
World's Columbian Exposition,
Chicago, 1893.*

I would reach for my own with joyful hands. It's a pleasure to be alive.

In the midst of the general characterlessness of the crafts we must recognize the great service of the two branches of the Austrian arts and crafts already mentioned. They had enough backbone not to conform to the general denial of the time. But respect must also be paid to the Viennese people, who, in spite of all the reforms in the arts and crafts, supported these two industries by their desire to buy. Today we may say confidently that it was only through the production of leather fancy-goods and through the gold and silver industries that the Austrian arts and crafts received recognition in the world market.

Indeed, the manufacturers in these industries did not wait until the state, by introducing the English models, ended the universal commercial stagnation—a step which now has proved necessary in the furniture industry—but rather, having already gathered new strength from the English ideas fifty years earlier, they were renewed and solidly established. For the furniture industry is English from A to Z. Yet despite this fact no decline has become noticeable, as had been prophesied by the pessimists in the furniture business. "England means the death of the arts and crafts." They say the death of the arts and crafts, but they mean of the acanthus ornament—about which it is probably true. But our time places more importance on correct form, solid materials, precise execution. *This is what is meant by arts and crafts!*

In the exhibition the gold- and silversmiths reveal that they are by no means free of the influence that emanates from the Stubenring.[2] They lack the courage of their convictions. The display windows on Kärntnerstrasse, on the Graben, and on the Kohlmarkt give us a better picture of the taste of the Viennese than does the silversmith's shop, where we can sense a certain fear that "up there" and among the other crafts the silversmiths will not maintain their status if they do not produce "stylish" things. But nevertheless there are still sufficient proofs of true craftsmanship, of independent workshop discoveries, of an art which is simple but which has the merit of having begun in the workshop and of having had nothing at all added to it from outside.

The leather workers are better off. They are still not so strongly dependent on the School of Applied Arts. And they owe their international reputation to the happy circumstance that the state has neglected to found a professional school specifically for their discipline. That's the only thing we are lacking. Just put the famous architect at their head, and then farewell, you old and honest handicraft tradition! The dilettantism of the drawing board would take possession of all forms, just as it did in the other hapless crafts that were destroyed in schools. The most ancient travel equipment would be reconstructed on the basis of manuscripts and monuments; the Austrian leather industry would succeed in making itself a laughingstock by manufacturing Gothic suitcases, Renaissance hatboxes, and Greek cigarette cases. But, of course, only at the Chicago Exposition, since these things could never have succeeded as export items.

To be well dressed—who does not want to be well dressed? Our century has done away with dress code regulations.[1] Everyone now enjoys the right to dress as he pleases, even like the king if he wants. The level of a nation's culture can be measured by how many of its citizens take advantage of this newly acquired freedom. In England and America, everyone does so; in the Balkan states, only the upper ten thousand. And in Austria? I do not care to hazard an answer to this question.

An American philosopher says somewhere, "A young man is rich if he has a good head on his shoulders and a good suit in the closet." That is sound philosophy. It demonstrates an understanding of people. What good are brains if they do not express themselves in good clothes? For both the English and the Americans demand of an individual that he be well dressed.

But the Germans do them one better. They also want to be *beautifully* dressed. When the English wear wide pants, the Germans point out to them immediately (I don't know whether this is thanks to old Vischer[2] or to the golden section) that these are unaesthetic and that only narrow pants may be considered to have any claim to *beauty*. They bluster, they grumble, and they curse, but nevertheless they have their trousers widened from year to year. They complain that fashion is just a tyrant. So it is; but what then? Has a reassessment of values been undertaken? The English once again are wearing a narrow cut of trousers, and now exactly the same arguments are being used to prove the *beauty* of wide pants. Let this be a lesson!

But the English mock the Germans' craving for beauty. The Medici Venus, the Pantheon, a picture by Botticelli, a song by Burns—of course, these are beautiful! But pants? Or whether a jacket has three or four buttons? Or whether the waistcoat is cut low or high? I don't know, but it makes me uneasy, it frightens me when I hear discussions about the beauty of such things. I get quite nervous when, gloating over another's deficiency, someone asks me in reference to a piece of clothing, "Is that supposed to be beautiful?"

Germans from the best society side with the English. They are satisfied if they are dressed *well*. They abjure claims to *beauty*. The great poet, the great painter, the great architect dress like the English. The would-be poet, the would-be master painter, the budding architect, on the other hand, make temples of their bodies in which beauty in the form of velvet collars, aesthetic trouser fabric, and Secessionist neckties is to be worshiped.

But what does it mean to be dressed well? It means to be dressed correctly.

To be dressed correctly! I feel as if I have revealed in these words the secret that has surrounded the fashion of our clothes up until now. We have tried to get at fashion with words like "beautiful," "stylish," "elegant," "smart," and "strong." But this is not the point. Rather, it is a question of being dressed *in such a way that one stands out the least*. A red dress coat stands out in a ballroom. It follows that a red dress coat is unmodern in the ballroom. A top hat stands out at the ice-skating rink. Consequently it is unmodern to wear a top hat while on the ice. In good society, to be conspicuous is bad manners.

However, this axiom is not equally practicable in every situation. A certain coat might go unnoticed in Hyde Park, but would be highly conspicuous in Peking, Zanzibar, or Vienna on the Stephansplatz. The coat is simply European. It is im-

5 Showroom of the Goldman & Salatsch menswear store, the Graben, Vienna. Interior by Adolf Loos, 1898. From Das Interieur: Wiener Monatshefte für Angewandte Kunst II, *Vienna, 1901.*

*I have already made several of these
ideas public in my lectures in the master
tailor course at the Museum of
Technological Trades.

TAILORS AND OUTFITTERS
GOLDMAN & SALATSCH

K. U. K. HOF-
LIEFERANTEN
K. BAYER. HOF-
LIEFERANTEN

KAMMER-
LIEFERANTEN
Sr. k. u. k. Hoheit des
Herrn Erzherzog Josef
etc. etc.

WIEN, I. GRABEN 20.

6

TAILORS AND OUTFITTERS
GOLDMAN & SALATSCH

K. U. K. HOF-
LIEFERANTEN
K. BAYER. HOF-
LIEFERANTEN

KAMMER-
LIEFERANTEN
Sr. k. u. k. Hoheit des
Herrn Erzherzog Josef
etc. etc.

WIEN, I. GRABEN 20.

7

possible to demand that the man at the height of fashion and culture dress in Peking like the Chinese, in Zanzibar like the East Africans, and on the Stephansplatz like the Viennese! The axiom must therefore be narrowed. In order to be dressed correctly, one must not stand out at *the center of culture.**

At the moment, the center of Western culture is London. Of course, it might certainly happen that during his wanderings the stroller would come upon surroundings with which he contrasted sharply. He would then have to change his coat as he passed from one street to another. This would not do. We may now formulate our precept in its most complete form. It goes like this: an article of clothing is modern when the wearer stands out as little as possible at the center of culture, on a specific occasion, *in the best society.* This is a very English axiom to which every fashionable intellectual would probably agree. But it meets with hearty opposition among the middle- and lower-class Germans. No nation has as many dandies as the German. A dandy is a man whose clothing serves only to distinguish him from his environment. Now ethics, now hygiene, now even aesthetics is adduced to attempt to explain the conduct of this kind of buffoon. There is a bond that links them all together; it runs from Master Diefenbach[3] to Professor Jager[4] through the "modern" would-be poet down to the Viennese landlord's son. But in spite of this they do not seem to get along. No dandy will admit to being one. One dandy mocks the other; under the pretext of attempting to exterminate the whole race of dandies, he continues to commit the sins of the breed. The modern dandy, or the dandy in general, is only one species of a far-reaching family.

The Germans suspect this dandy of setting the trend in the affairs of men's fashion. But this is flattering the poor creature far more than he deserves. We have already seen that it cannot even be said of the dandy that he dresses in a modern way. That would be of no use to him. For the dandy always wears only that which *the society around him* considers modern.

Yes, but is this not the same as being dressed in a modern way? By no means. This is why the dandies in every city look different. That which in city A creates quite a stir has already lost its excitement in city B. The darling of fashion in Berlin runs the risk of being scoffed at in Vienna. But well-heeled circles will always give priority to those shifts in fashion of which the middle classes take the least notice. No longer protected by dress regulations, they do not like being imitated by someone on the very next day. And so it is necessary to begin casting about for a substitute immediately. But only the most discreet means will be used in this eternal pursuit of materials and styles. The new cut will be kept for years like an open secret of the great tailors, only to be let out in the end by some fashion magazine. Then it still takes a few years until everyone, down to the very last man in the country, knows about it. And this is where the dandies have their day; they take over the whole affair. But the original cut has now changed quite a bit in the course of its long travels; it has adapted to specific geographical situations.

You can count on the fingers of one hand the great tailors worldwide who are in the position to dress one according to the most elegant principles. In fact, there are some metropolises in the old world which are unable to point to a single firm of this kind. There wasn't even one in Berlin until a Viennese master, E. Ebenstein, established a branch there. Before that the Berlin court was forced to have a good part of its wardrobe made at Poole's in London. But we possess a large selection of this small group of firms here in Vienna. We owe this happy circumstance to the fact that our nobility has a standing invitation to the drawing

12

8

room of the Queen; they have had many of their things made in England and have thus transplanted that elegant tone in clothing back to Vienna. It was in this way that the Viennese tailors attained their enviable position. One could probably say that on the Continent the top ten thousand best-dressed men are in Vienna, for even the lesser tailors are raised to a higher level by these great firms.

The great firms, as well as their closest imitators and competitors, all have one feature in common: they fear the public eye. Wherever possible, they limit themselves to a small circle of customers. Of course, they are not as exclusive as some of the houses in London, where admittance is conditional upon a personal recommendation by the Prince of Wales. But all public ostentation is anathema. It was the difficult task of the directors of the exhibition to induce some of the best Viennese houses to display their products. And it is clear that they slipped out of this noose quite cleverly. They exhibited only those objects which precluded imitation. Ebenstein was the most clever. He exhibited a tuxedo (incorrectly identified here in Vienna as a smoking jacket) designed for the tropics (!), a hunting vest, a Prussian commander's military uniform for ladies, and a coaching coat with engraved mother-of-pearl buttons, each of which was a masterpiece in itself. A. Keller displayed, in addition to his other excellent uniforms, a dress coat with the obligatory gray trousers; one could journey to England quite comfortably in this outfit. The Norfolk jacket also seemed to be well made. Uzel & Son showed the specialty of their workshop: uniforms for court and state occasions. They really must be quite fine; otherwise the firm could not have maintained its leading position in this line of business for such a long time. Franz Bubacek displayed hunting clothes for the kaiser. The cut of the Norfolk jacket is fashionable and correct. Herr Bubacek is making quite a show of courage by displaying it; he is not afraid of imitators. You can say the same of Goldman & Salatsch; they were there with their specialty, uniforms for the naval squadrons.

But this is the end of my unqualified praise. The collective exhibit of the Union of Viennese Clothing Makers does not warrant it. Industries that cater to the general public must often look the other way, since the customer, by insisting on the fulfillment of his own desires, is frequently responsible for many a tasteless product. But here is precisely where the craftsmen could have shown that they were above their clientele; they could have taken up the banner against the large firms and then would have been left to do as they liked. But most have let this opportunity slip. They already reveal their ignorance in the choice of material. They make overcoats out of covercoat material and vice versa. They make lounge suits out of Norfolk material, frock coats out of smooth cloth.

They hardly do better with the cut of the clothes. Very few start out from the standpoint of working in an elegant style; most of them turn to the dandies for their inspiration. Of course, that kind of person can afford to indulge in double-breasted waistcoats and checked suits with velvet collars! One firm went so far as to produce a jacket with blue velvet cuffs! Well, if *that* isn't modern . . .

But I will mention here a few who have managed to keep their distance from this witches' sabbath. Anton Adam does good work, but cuts his waistcoats a little too low. Alexander Deutsch showed a nice winter overcoat, Joseph Hummel a nice ulster; P. Kroupa ruins his otherwise correct frock coat with braided trimming. There is one other firm that exhibited its products openly at the show which I would like to have mentioned. But when I attempted to open up a pleat on a Norfolk jacket that was ostensibly there to afford additional freedom of movement for the arm, I was unable to do so. It was counterfeit.

9 Tailor's pattern for a Norfolk jacket. From J. P. Thornton, The Sectional System of Gentlemen's Garment Cutting, Comprising Coats, Vests, Breeches, and Trousers, London, 1887.

I regret that I am unable to praise everything all the time. I feel obliged now and again to say a word of criticism. But I can gather from the many letters that I have received that people hold this need of mine against me. Of course, the Viennese crafts industry is not used to being criticized seriously. And this is much to its detriment. The many laudatory articles which so often greet the opening of these exhibitions have had a debilitating, hothouse effect on the crafts. It is feared that a slight breeze will harm the spoiled little darling, that he will catch cold in the draft. If I were really convinced of this, I would let the winds blow! But I believe that the child was born of sturdy parents and that rather than cause harm, the little bit of breeze can do him a lot of good. It will even help to harden him up some.

Many of my ideas will stir up quite a bit of consternation. I am looking at the exhibition as a foreigner, not as someone from Vienna. And deliberately so. For I am writing with reference to the Paris World's Fair.[1] I am trying to make those in the Vienna crafts industry aware of the products that they now produce merely as a matter of course. They do not even consider them worthy of exhibition, although these are the products that the rest of the world sees as unsurpassable. But at the same time the Viennese must be cautioned against displaying in Paris those of their products that are made with greater skill abroad.

But does the crafts industry itself not know what its best products are? Oh no. It knows as little about its own production as the poet, the painter, in fact, any artist at all can know about his own art. Such an artist will always value most highly those products of his muse which have cost him the most effort and vexation. Those creations, however, which he produced almost naturally, without effort, to which he was predisposed and which bear most strongly the stamp of his own individuality, his own character—these he dismisses as not particularly important. Only the unanimous agreement of his public is able to convey to him the correct opinion of his products. But the artist in Vienna has very seldom listened to the opinions of London, Paris, and New York. And it seems to me that the right moment has come for listening, now, at the end of the century, since he is preparing to open his mind to these opinions. In Paris we should show people what we can do and not what we wish we were able to do. To exhibit the latter would do us very little good. It is preferable to display objects that are perhaps less artistic but of which, even if just by a subtle nuance, no one can see better examples in another exhibit.

It is in Paris that the most burning question of our time will probably be solved, the one that is worrying the crafts industry at present: which will prevail, the old style or the modern style? Other nations of culture have long since taken a decisive stand on the matter and will command attention in Paris through their definitive and firm positions. Even the Germans, who arrived in Chicago with great fanfare, withdrew discreetly when they realized that the great hullabaloo was inappropriate and that they still had much to learn from the Americans— even the German nation, which lagged behind for so long, has joined the other peoples of culture enthusiastically. We alone still remain backward, so backward in fact that when Hofrat von Scala[2] offered the crafts industry a helping hand, its members were contrary enough to turn it down and to go ahead and found a new newspaper of their own in order to combat the new tendency. In Germany over the past few months four journals have been started to propagate the new style; if someone were to publish an adversary paper in Germany it would probably be received with excessive serenity. We are no more stupid than our neighbors. On the contrary! We in fact have something which most people lack: our cele-

The New Style and the Bronze Industry

Neue Freie Presse, *May 29, 1898*

10 Entry of the Austrian Exhibition at the Universal Exposition of 1900 in Paris. From Innen Dekoration, *vol. 11, Darmstadt, September 1900.*

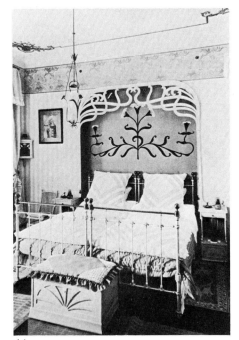

11

12

13

brated Viennese good taste, of which some could even be jealous. It is only those unreasonable schools of ours which are to be blamed. They have inhibited the natural development of our arts and crafts.

But the answer to that persistent question goes like this: everything that an earlier period has already produced, insofar as it is still useful today, can be imitated. But the new phenomena of our culture (railroad cars, telephones, typewriters, and so forth) must be resolved without any conscious echoes of a formal style that has already been superseded. Modifications of old objects in order to assimilate them to modern uses are not permitted. And so the rule is this: either imitate or create something that is totally new. Of course, I do not necessarily mean by this that that which is new is always the opposite of that which came before.

As far as I know, this challenge has never before been expressed so exactly and so precisely, even though similar statements have been made abroad in professional circles and even recently in the Austrian Museum. But people have actually been working according to this principle for years now. And this is perfectly comprehensible. A copy of an old master is also a work of art. Who can forget Lenbach's magnificent imitations of old Italian masters in the Schack Gallery in Munich?[3] But what is totally unworthy of being called a true work of art is the conscious effort to express new ideas in the style of an old master. It is destined to fail. This is not to say that a modern artist, through an extensive study of a particular school, through a predilection and reverence for a particular period or master, cannot make that style so much his own that his work strongly bears the spiritual imprint of his master. I only have to think of the old-master feeling in Lenbach, or the Quattrocento pictures by the English. But the true artist cannot paint now *à la* Botticelli, now *à la* Titian, and now *à la* Raphael Mengs.

What would one think of a writer who today wrote a play in the style of Aeschylus, tomorrow composed a poem in the style of Gerhart Hauptmann, and the day after tomorrow, a farce in the style of Hans Sachs? And worse, what writer would have the pitiful courage to reveal his own impotence by confessing his sources? And now let us consider a state school for poets where young artists would be emasculated by being constrained to follow this doctrine of counterfeit, where this kind of literary servitude would be raised to a principle. The whole world would pity the victims of such a method. Yet such a school exists, not for poets, but for the arts and crafts.

Of course, when we copy an object, we must not change it in any way. And yet, inasmuch as we have very little respect for our own time, we likewise have very little for earlier periods. We can always find in an older piece of work something to criticize. And we delude ourselves in the happy belief that we are able to do better. Thus we hounded the German Renaissance to death with talk of "beautiful" proportions. It was necessary to make alterations, to "beautify" the style, as it was put. But after all these years, we see that these supposed beautifications were not improvements at all; the old model or an exact copy of it shines in its originality, while the poor imitation has become unbearable with its innumerable "beautifications." And is this supposed to be a salutary lesson for the crafts industry? By no means! The craftsman only draws the conclusion from all of this that the beautifications were not radical enough! For the old object is far from being to his taste. Once again he knows how to make new improvements. And after some years, the cycle begins all over again. And it would have continued in the same way up to this very day if the new head of the Austrian Museum had not put an end to this more comic than tragic labor of Sisyphus. From now on objects which are in any style other than that of the Stubenring and which the producers wish to exhibit must be exact imitations.

As a consequence of this dictum, how does our bronze industry stand now? Very differently. Those articles which have been withdrawn from the jurisdiction of the schools are again, naturally, the best. Perhaps it is for this reason that they fail to be exhibited. I am talking about those charming bronze knickknacks in natural colors, a Viennese speciality, which are the delight of every *flâneur* along the Graben. Here, under Japanese influence, we can see the birth of something authentically Viennese, about which we are justified in feeling proud. Yet as much as I have asked around, I have received from everyone the same answer: no one has any room for these "ordinary" things. Everyone points with great satisfaction, however, to the works of art that they have acquired for the exhibition from the most renowned architects and professors. These renowned gentlemen abused each and every style.

The School of Applied Arts sets the fashion for useful objects. In Vienna it is no easy task to get hold of a good coal scuttle or fireplace fender! And how difficult it is to find good hardware for doors and windows! I once wrote somewhere that in the last two decades we have successively gotten Renaissance, Baroque, and Rococo blisters on our hands because of our door handles. There is, however, *one* proper door handle in Vienna to which I have access; I make a pilgrimage to it whenever I am in the neighborhood. It is located in the new building on the Kohlmarkt and was designed by Professor König. But do not go there, my dear reader! They would suspect that I was teasing them if you did. That is how unobtrusive this handle is.

Thank God there is one noteworthy display of patented walking sticks and umbrellas at the exhibition, by the firm of Balduin Heller Sons, which does not show any ornament. For this reason I cannot recommend it enough. At a time when every door latch, every picture frame, every inkwell, every coal shovel, every corkscrew makes such a hullabaloo, such an attempt at modesty deserves double support.

But the brass beds that we first began to adopt from the English a few years ago because we enjoyed their noble simplicity so much have now acclimated best of all and shout for attention in competition with the latches, frames, shovels, and all the rest.

11 *"Modern bedroom in the English style." Keller & Reiner showroom, Berlin. From* Innen Dekoration, *vol. 10, October 1899.*
12 *Bedroom furniture of polished maple, designed by Adolf Loos for the apartment of Eugen Stössler. From* Das Interieur I, *1900.*
13 *Door handle, Manz bookstore, Kohlmarkt, Vienna. Adolf Loos, 1910.*

14 So-called Gschnaszimmer *or*
"carnival room" of Fürstin Pauline
Metternich, Vienna, c. 1890.

The carpenters have displayed their products to the right and to the left of the silver courtyard. Stalls were constructed and model rooms were built in them. This is how it has been done for years at every exhibition. Thus the carpenters say to their clients: This is how you should live!

The poor client! He is not permitted to arrange his own living space by himself. That would be a pretty mess. He would not know where to begin. The "stylish" home, that great conquest of our century, demands extraordinary knowledge and know-how.

It was not always like this. Up until the beginning of this century people did not have these concerns. One purchased furniture from the carpenter, wallpaper from the paperhanger, lamp fittings from the bronze founder, and so on. And if they did not all fit together? This could happen. But one did not let himself get carried away by such problems. In those days one decorated his home the way one outfits himself today. We buy our shoes from the shoemaker, coat, pants, and waistcoat from the tailor, collars and cuffs from the shirtmaker, hats from the hatter, and walking stick from the turner. None of them knows any of the others, and yet everything matches quite nicely. How can this be? It happens because all of them work in the style of 1898. The craftsmen in the home-furnishing industry also used to work in this way in earlier times, everyone in one style, the one which currently prevailed—the modern style.

But then, all of a sudden, the modern style developed a bad reputation. It would be too complex to explain why in these pages. Suffice it to say that men became dissatisfied with their times. To be modern, to think and feel in the modern way, was considered superficial. The profound individual sought to immerse himself in another era; he found happiness for himself as an ancient Greek or as a medieval metaphysician or as a Renaissance man.

This fraudulence was of course too much for the honest craftsman. He was unable to participate in it. He understood too well how people ought to store their clothes in a wardrobe and how his fellow men wanted to take a rest. But now he was expected to make all kinds of chests and chairs for his customers—Greek, Roman, Gothic, Moorish, Italian, German, Baroque, classical—according to their respective spiritual creeds. Moreover, one room was to be decorated in one style, the next in another. As I said, the craftsman just could not keep up with it.

Then he was placed under tutelage. And he still finds himself in that position today. At first the scholarly archaeologist set himself up as the craftsman's tutor. But that did not last for long. Then came the upholsterer; no one could have held much against him since he had had very little to do in preceding centuries and thus could not very well be restrained from imitating old models. He seized the advantage and flooded the market with innumerable new forms. He made furniture that was so totally overstuffed that the cabinetmaker's woodwork could no longer be seen. These pieces were hailed with great shouts of joy. The public had by now had enough of archaeology; people were pleased finally to get furniture in their homes that belonged to their own era, that appeared to be modern. The upholsterer, that worthy man, at an earlier time had industriously stitched away with his needle and stuffed his mattresses. Now he let his hair grow long, donned a velvet jacket, tied around his neck a tie that fluttered as he walked, and became an artist. He removed the word "cushion-maker" from the firm's sign and substituted "decorator" for it. It had a better ring.

And so the domination by the upholsterers began; it was a reign of terror that we can all still feel in our bones. Velvet and silk, silk and velvet, Makart bouquets,[1] dust, suffocating air and lack of light, portieres, carpets, and "arrangements"— thank God, we are done with all that now!

But then the cabinetmakers received a new tutor. This was the architect. He was well versed in the specialized literature and thus was easily able to carry out all commissions involving his expertise in every sort of style. Would you like to have a Baroque bedroom? He will produce a Baroque bedroom for you. A Chinese spittoon? He will make one for you. He can do everything, everything, and in every style. He can design any useful object, from any period or people. The key to the secret of his uncanny productive ability lies in a piece of tracing paper. Right after he has secured a commission, he sets out with his tracing paper for the library of the School of Applied Arts—if, that is, he has not indebted himself to the local bookseller for the sake of his own larger private library. In the afternoons he sits glued to the seat of his drawing board and traces a Baroque bedroom or a Chinese spittoon.

But the rooms of these architects had one flaw. They were not cozy enough. They were naked and cold. Where there had only been fabric before, now there were only profiles, columns, and cornices. Then the upholsterer was brought in again; he hung up coziness by the yard on the doors and windows. But alas, to look at the rooms when the net curtains and the portieres had to be taken down to be cleaned. No one could stand it for very long in the bare rooms. The lady of the house was embarrassed down to the depths of her soul to have to receive visitors during those times when coziness and intimacy were out at the cleaner's. It was all the stranger because the Renaissance, after which these rooms were modeled for the most part, did not have this convenience. And yet the coziness of Renaissance rooms had become proverbial.

The architect still plays the dominant role here today, but we see how the painter and the sculptor are gradually preparing to take his place, to become his successor. Will they perform any better? I do not think so. The carpenter cannot put up with any tutor, and it is high time for this completely unjustified and imposed tutelage to be abolished. Of course, we must not then expect the impossible from our carpenter. He speaks German, the German of Vienna in 1898. Do not rebuke him as stupid or inept if he cannot speak Middle High German, French, Russian, Chinese, and Greek simultaneously. Of course he cannot. But he is also a little out of practice in his own native language since he has been kept down for nearly half a century now and made to parrot back all the manners of speech dictated to him. Do not demand from him a virtuoso performance right away in his own language. Give him time slowly to get acquainted with it again.

I am well aware that such words are of little use to either the carpenter or the general public. The craftsman has been so intimidated by his long years of dependence on a tutor that he does not trust himself to step forward with his own ideas. And the public is intimidated in exactly the same way. Hofrat von Scala, the director of the Austrian Museum, has attempted to intervene, however, in a useful and supportive way. He demonstrated by the example of English furniture, which he had copied, that the public may also buy furniture that has been felt by the carpenter, conceived by the carpenter, and made by the carpenter. These pieces of furniture had no profile and no pillars; they were effective simply because of their comfort, their solid material, and their precise workmanship. They were Viennese cigarette boxes translated into the language of the car-

15 Lusterweibchen, *Franz Barwig, Vienna. A* Lusterweibchen *is a chandelier that typically combines the antlers of a deer and a wood-carved female figure bearing candles. From* Blätter für Kunstgewerbe: Organ des Wiener Kunstgewerbe-Vereins, *vol. 7, Vienna, 1898.*

penter. Many a master craftsman must have thought to himself at the time, I could really make that kind of chair myself without the help of any architects! Just a few more Christmas exhibitions like this and we will have a different generation of carpenters. The public is already there, awaiting the things to come.

Yes, the public is waiting. I am convinced of it by the countless letters I receive with their requests for names of craftsmen who work in the modern style. "Please send me reliable information with the addresses of several furniture houses that follow the progressive recommendations made by Hofrat von Scala. I am planning to furnish a salon, but wherever I ask, they always recommend to me Louis XV, Louis XVI, Empire, and the like." Such are the complaints I receive from the provinces. It sets one to thinking.

In the assembly room of the Crafts Association, the Viennese arts and crafts workers were voicing their complaints. It was all Hofrat von Scala's fault. "You see, Herr Architect," said one craftsman to me after the meeting, "we are having a pretty bad time of it. The good times that we had are gone. Twenty years ago I could sell a *lusterweibchen* for a hundred gulden. And do you know how much I get for the very same *lusterweibchen* today?" He named a figure that was really quite low. I felt sorry for the man. He seemed possessed by the notion that he would have to make *lusterweibchen* all his life. If only someone could convince him otherwise. For people do not want *lusterweibchen* anymore. They want what is new, new, new. And that is truly lucky for our crafts industry. The taste of the public is in constant flux. Modern products will fetch the highest prices, unmodern products the lowest. So, craftsmen of Vienna, you have a choice! But those of you who regard the modern movement with fear simply because your storerooms are full of unmodern furniture do not have the right to oppose this movement. Least of all do you have the right to demand from the head of a state institution like the Austrian Museum, which must protect the interests of all craftsmen, that a position be taken that would facilitate the sale of your furniture stocks. A servant of the state may not get involved in such affairs.

Today I wish to speak only of the surroundings that the carpenters of Vienna have chosen for their products in the Rotunda. The Carpenters Association is in very mediocre surroundings, the Arts and Crafts Division of the Lower Austrian Crafts Union in excellent ones. Do not object that the one cost more than the other. The architect of the Arts and Crafts Division could never have managed to mount stone-engraved Roman capital letters on wooden boards, the pretty effect of which, moreover, was heightened by the artistry of the painter. Imitative two times over! And the Viennese unfortunately are already so far along their merry way that they do not even let this simple counterfeit pass. The architect Pletschnik,[2] however, to whom the Vienna Crafts Association offered the opportunity to express his extraordinary ability—an offer for which all modern-thinking people are indebted—acquitted himself of the task in an unusual way. Pervading this exhibit is a touch of elegance, for which the objects displayed unfortunately cannot take credit; they are too uneven in quality. The individual stalls are framed with dark green velvet, to which a decoration cut out of pasteboard and covered with light green silk is attached. Its effect is heightened extraordinarily by silver disks and silver letters. The whole display is spanned by a white canopy with a dull violet ornament, the first satisfactory solution to the problem of canopy decoration in Vienna. Elaborate lacework conceals the incandescent lamps. A charming and unique effect. A red carpet underfoot. One has only to observe the public. With what reverence it traverses these rooms. Even the doormats are used with zeal.

16 Central room of the Arts and Crafts Division at the Vienna Jubilee Exhibition. Josef Pletschnik, 1898. From Ver Sacrum: Organ der Vereinigung Bildender Künstler Oesterreichs, *no. 1, Vienna, October 1898.*

The demands I put forth in the preceding article amount to heresy. Neither the archaeologist nor the interior decorator nor the architect nor the painter nor the sculptor should design our homes. Well, who should do it then? The answer is very simple: everyone should be his own decorator.

Then, of course, we would not be able to live in "stylish" homes. But this "style," style in quotation marks, is not really necessary. What is this style anyway? It is hard to define. In my opinion the best answer to the question of what stylish is was given by that stout housewife who said, "When there is a lion's head on the night table, and when this same lion's head is present on the sofa, the chest, the beds, the chairs, the washstand, in short, on all objects in the room, then one calls this room stylish." Cross your heart, my dear craftsmen, can you honestly say that you did not contribute to teaching the people to have such a nonsensical opinion? It was not always a lion's head. But a column, a knob, or a balustrade was always forced upon all the furniture; at times it was a longer one, at times a shorter one, at times a thicker, at times a thinner one.

This kind of room tyrannized its poor inhabitants. Alas, pity the unfortunate owner who ventured to purchase something additional for it! For this furniture can tolerate absolutely nothing else in its vicinity. If one received something as a gift, there was no place to put it. And if one moved to a new place that did not have exactly the same dimensions as the old one, then one had to give up forever the idea of having a "stylish" home. Then the Old German ornamental divan[1] would perhaps have to be put in the blue Rococo salon and the Baroque chest in the Empire sitting room. What a horror!

Compared with this, the ignorant peasant, the poor worker, and the old maid were well off. They did not have problems like these. Their homes were not stylishly decorated. One piece came from here, another from there. Everything was mixed together. But how can this be explained? The painters, whom one credited with having some amount of taste, neglected our magnificent homes and painted instead interiors for the ignorant peasants, the poor workers, and the old maids. But how could anyone find these interiors beautiful? For we have been taught that only "stylish" homes are beautiful.

But the painters were right. Thanks to their trained and practiced vision, they have a sharper eye than other men for all the externalities of life. They recognized the emptiness, the puffed-up posturing, the strangeness and disharmony of our stylish homes. People are not comfortable in these rooms, and the rooms are not suitable for people. And how could they be? The architect, the interior decorator, hardly even knows his customer's name. And even if the occupant of these rooms has paid for them a hundred times over, they are still not *his* rooms. They remain forever the spiritual possession of the person who has conceived them. Nor could they have any real effect on the painters. They lacked any spiritual relation to the person who occupied them; they lacked that certain something that the painters found in the room of the ignorant peasant, the poor worker, and the old maid: they lacked intimacy.

I did not grow up, thank God, in a stylish home. At that time no one knew what it was yet. Now, unfortunately, everything is different in my family too. But in those days! Here was the table, a totally crazy and intricate piece of furniture, an extension table with a shocking bit of work as a lock. But it was *our* table, *ours!* Can you understand what that means? Do you know what wonderful times we had there? Evenings, when I was a young boy and the lamp was burning, I was

Interiors in the Rotunda

Neue Freie Presse, *June 12, 1898*

17 Bedroom of Otto Wagner's apartment at 3 Rennweg, Vienna. Otto Wagner, 1897. From Einige Skizzen, Projekte, und Ausgeführte Bauwerke von Otto Wagner, *vol. 2, Vienna, 1897.*

never able to tear myself away from it! Father always imitated the night watchman's horn so that I would run—terrified—into my bedroom. And there was the writing table! There was an ink stain on it; my sister Hermine had knocked over the inkwell when she was a little baby. And there was the picture of my parents! What a hideous frame! But it was a wedding gift from the workers at my father's shop. And that old-fashioned chair! A leftover from my grandmother's household. A knit slipper in which one could hang the clock—my sister Irma had made it in kindergarten. Every piece of furniture, every thing, every object had a story to tell, a family history. The house was never finished; it grew along with us and we grew within it. Of course it did not have any style to it. That means there was no strangeness, no age. But there was one style that our home did have—the style of its occupants, the style of our family.

When the times in their ever more dictatorial way demanded "stylish" homes—everyone we knew had already decorated their homes in Old German, and one could not lag behind—then all of the "old junk" was thrown away. Pieces of junk they were only to the stranger; they were holy relics to the family. Only one thing remained—the wallpaper.

But now we have had enough. We want to rule again within our own four walls. If we do not have any taste, then good, our homes will be tastelessly decorated. If we do have taste, so much the better. We will not allow ourselves to be tyrannized by our rooms any longer. We will buy everything together, everything whenever and wherever we can use it, just as we please.

Just as we please! Yes, then we might acquire that style for which we have been searching for such a long time, with which we have always wanted to fill our rooms. The style that not lions' heads, but the good taste or, for all I care, bad taste of an individual or a family has produced. The common bond that ties all of the furniture in one room together consists in the fact that the owner has made the selection. And even if he should proceed in an illogical manner, especially in the choice of colors, it would still be no misfortune. A home that has grown together with a family can withstand a great deal. When, on the other hand, one puts even one extra knickknack that does not belong there in a "stylish room," the entire room can be "ruined." In the family's room, however, every new piece is absorbed immediately and completely into the space. Such a room is like a violin. One can get to know a violin by practicing on it, a room by living in it.

Naturally rooms that are not used for living are not relevant to this discussion. I will let the plumber take care of the powder room and the bathroom; the appropriate specialist will see to the kitchen. And finally, for those rooms used for the reception of guests, for celebrations, and for extraordinary occasions, I will call in the architect, the painter, the sculptor, the interior decorator. Every individual will find someone who fulfills his specific needs. For there is always a spiritual bond between the producer and the consumer of goods, but it surely cannot be extended to rooms that are for living.

It has always been this way. Even the king lived in a room that developed with and through him. But he received guests in rooms that were created by the court architects. And when the good subjects were led through the golden rooms, this sigh escaped many a breast: "Oh, he has it good! If only I could live as well as he does!" For the worthy subjects are unable to imagine their king other than dressed in a crimson ermine coat, with a scepter in his hand and a crown on his head, strolling in his park. No wonder that the good subject, as soon as he came

*18 Salon of Otto Wagner's apartment
at 3 Rennweg, with view into bedroom.
Otto Wagner, 1897. From* Einige
Skizzen, Projekte, und Ausgeführte
Bauwerke von Otto Wagner, *vol. 2,
1897.*

into money, immediately went about securing for himself too these presumably royal living quarters. I am actually astonished that I haven't yet seen anyone running around dressed in crimson!

Slowly but surely, however, it was discovered with dismay that in fact even the king lives quite simply. The retreat was abrupt. Simplicity was the last word, even in ballrooms. In other countries, the march of fashion is once again beginning to advance, while we are just preparing to retreat. There is no escape from it, no matter how much—alas, very, very much!—our craftsmen would like. Taste and the desire for variety always go hand in hand. Today we wear narrow pants, tomorrow wide ones, the day after tomorrow, it's back to the narrow style again. Every tailor knows this. Yes, you will say, but we could spare ourselves the next wave of wide pants. Oh no! We need them so that we will be glad to get back to narrow ones again. We need a period of simple ballrooms in order to prepare ourselves for the return of the elaborate ballroom. If our craftsmen want to get over the period of simplicity more quickly, there is only one way: to accept it.

At present we are just entering upon this period. One can tell that this is the case from the fact that the most admired room in the Rotunda is also the simplest one. It is a bedroom with bath, specifically intended for the designer himself. It is my belief that this may be the reason that the public is so strongly attracted to this room; they queue up to see it. The room pulses with all the magic of the individual and the personal. No one could ever live in it, no one could occupy it, be totally and completely alive in it, other than the owner himself: Otto Wagner.

Hofrat Exner[2] secured the room immediately for the Paris World's Fair. There it will have the function of fooling the Parisians into thinking that all of the Viennese bathe and sleep this way. Between you and me, we can admit, of course, that we have not come this far yet. But this room will cause a great upheaval in our home-furnishing trade. For, as I have pointed out before, people like it. The Austrian Museum prepared the way well with its Christmas Exhibition. Just think, now the Viennese even find a brass bed to be beautiful. Nothing elaborate, just the simplest bed that one can imagine. And the upholsterer has not even made an attempt to conceal the bars with fabric as was always the case before. That is, brass beds always had to be "padded." A smooth and polished green paneled wall encloses the room; valuable engravings punctuate the space. An ottoman covered with a polar bear skin, two brass night tables, two cupboards and two cabinets, a table, two armchairs, and several other chairs fill the room. Cherry-tree branches are embroidered naturalistically on the cloth wallpaper on top of the paneled walls. The canopy over the bed is decorated in the same way. The ceiling is whitewashed; incandescent lamps hang at the end of silk ropes from the ceiling and are arranged in a circular pattern. The impression produced by the colors—evoked through the green wood, yellow brass, white fur, and red cherries—is extraordinary. I will refrain here from discussing the chairs in the room. But let it just be said that the carpet is not right. We have completely done away with the rose borders over which we had to stumble in earlier days. I do not think that the impression which this carpet gives of exposed roots, over which one might well trip, is any more agreeable. The problem is that the cherry tree is sending its roots out over the whole floor.

The bath is a jewel. The wall cladding, the floor covering, the ottoman cover, and the pillows are all made out of the same downy material as our bathrobes. It has been kept to a subdued violet pattern; the white, the purple, and the silver of the nickel-plated furniture, toiletry articles, and bathtub provide the dominant color

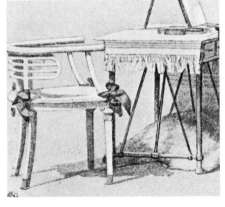

19 Bathroom furniture, Otto Wagner, 1898. It was shown at the Secession Exhibition in the Rotunda during the Vienna Jubilee. From Ver Sacrum, *no. 1, October 1898.*

scheme. The bathing unit is actually made out of plate-glass mounted with nickel. Even the cut-crystal faceted glasses on the washstand have been made according to Wagner's designs, as have the attractive fixtures, of course.

I am an opponent of the trend that considers it to be especially desirable that a building has been designed along with everything in it—down to the coal scoop—by the hand of one architect. I am of the opinion that the building can have a rather monotonous appearance as a result. All individuality is lost in the process. But I draw the line at the genius of Otto Wagner. For Otto Wagner has one quality that I have found in only a small number of English and American architects: he is able to slip out of his architect's skin and into the skin of any craftsman he chooses. When he makes a water glass, he thinks like a glass blower or a glass cutter. When he makes a brass bed, he thinks, he feels, like a worker in brass. All of the rest—his very great architectural knowledge and skill—has been left in the old skin. He takes only one thing with him wherever he goes: his artistry.

The Otto Wagner room is beautiful not because, but in spite of the fact that it was designed by an architect. For this architect served as his own decorator. This room will not suit any other person because it will not correspond to his personality. It lacks perfection for any second party; thus we may no longer speak of beauty. To do so really seems a contradiction.

By beauty we understand the highest degree of perfection. For this reason it is completely out of the question for anything impractical to be beautiful. The fundamental requirement for any object that would lay claim to the designation "beautiful" is that it not violate the boundaries of functionality. Of course, the functional object by itself is not beautiful. There is more to it than that. A Cinquecento theoretician of art probably expressed it most precisely. He said, "An object that is so perfect that one can neither add to it nor take away from it without harming it is beautiful. Only then does it possess the most perfect, the most complete harmony."

The beautiful man? He is the most perfect man, the man whose bodily structure and intellectual capacities offer the best assurance for healthy offspring and for the maintenance and sustenance of a family. The beautiful woman? She is the perfect woman. It is her responsibility to kindle a man's love for her, to nurse her children, and to give them a good upbringing. Thus she has the most beautiful eyes—practical, sharp (not short-sighted or timid), the most beautiful face, the most beautiful hair, the most beautiful nose—a nose that allows her to breathe well. She has the most beautiful mouth, the most beautiful teeth—teeth with which she can chew her food best. Nothing in nature is extraneous. The highest degree of functionality in harmony with all the other parts is what we call pure beauty.

We thus see that the beauty of a useful object only exists in relation to its purpose. There is no absolute beauty for the useful object. "See there, what a beautiful desk!" "The desk? Why, it's ugly!" "It's not a desk at all! It's a billiard table!" "Oh, a billiard table. Of course! It's a beautiful billiard table." "Look! What a lovely pair of sugar tongs!" "What, you think they are beautiful? I find them abominable!" "But it's a coal scoop!" "Well then, of course, it's a lovely coal scoop!" "What an exquisite bedroom Mr. X has!" (Substitute here the name of the stupidest man you know.) "What? Mr. X's bedroom? And you find that exquisite?" "Oh, I've made a mistake, it belongs to Oberbaurat[1] Otto Wagner, the greatest architect of his time." "But then of course it is exquisite, in fact." The most beautiful and most picturesque osteria with the most authentic dirt is ugly to anyone other than the Italian peasant. And these others are correct as far as they themselves are concerned.

So it goes for every single functional object. Are, for example, the chairs in the Wagner room beautiful? I do not think so because I cannot sit comfortably on them. Probably many others will discover the same thing. But it is perfectly possible that Otto Wagner can sit quite comfortably on these chairs. Thus in his bedroom, that is, a room where he does not receive guests, the chairs are beautiful (provided, of course, that he finds them comfortable). They are shaped like the Greek chairs. But over the course of the centuries the technique of sitting, the technique of being at rest, has undergone significant changes. It has never stood still. Every nation and every era have done it differently. Positions that for us would be exceedingly taxing for repose (just think of the Orientals) may for others be very practicable.

Furniture for Sitting

Neue Freie Presse, *June 19, 1898*

20 Accounting office of Goldman & Salatsch menswear store, the Graben, Vienna. Adolf Loos, 1898. From Das Interieur II, *1901.*

*21 Billiard room of the Museum
Cafe, Operngasse, Vienna. Adolf
Loos, 1899. From* Kunst und
Handwerk, *vol. 51, Munich, 1900.*

*22 Restaurant interior renovation by
Hans Mayr, with Loos's Museum
Cafe chairs, Kärntnerstrasse,
Vienna, 1902. From* Das Interieur
III, *1902.*

23 Chair designed by Adolf Loos for the Museum Cafe, Operngasse, Vienna, 1899. Manufactured by Thonet.

At present we demand from a chair not only that we may rest while sitting on it, but moreover that we may become rested *quickly* while sitting on it. "Time is money." Resting thus had to become a specialized field. Resting after an intellectual endeavor demands a totally different position from relaxing after outdoor exercise. Resting after doing gymnastics is different from resting after riding a horse; resting after riding a bike differs from resting after rowing a boat. Yes, and what is more, the degree to which one has exerted oneself demands its own particular technique of relaxation. One can expedite his relaxation by taking advantage of various opportunities to sit down, utilizing one after the other, and by finding a number of different attitudes and positions for the body. Have you never felt the need, especially if you are very tired, to hang one leg over the arm of a chair? In and of itself, this position is a very uncomfortable one, but sometimes it is a real boon. In America they are able to take advantage of it any time at all since no one there would ever consider a comfortable sitting position (and thus quick relaxation) impolite. There one is permitted to put his feet up on a table if the table is not used for meals. But in this country we seem to find it an affront when our fellow men make themselves comfortable. There are still people who become quite nervous in the presence of someone who puts his feet up on the opposite seat in a train compartment or lies down at all.

The English and Americans, who are free from such a petty way of thinking, have really perfected the art of relaxation. They have invented more kinds of chairs in the course of this century than the whole rest of the world, including all its various peoples, throughout its entire existence. According to the principle that every type of exertion demands a different chair, the English room never contains one consistent type of chair. All of the different possibilities for sitting are represented in one and the same room. Every individual can choose the seat that suits him best. The sole exception is those rooms which are used only from time to time and which at those times demand that all of the occupants use the room for the same purpose: the ballroom, for example, or the dining room. But the drawing room, what we call the "salon," provides easily movable seats that are suitable to the function of the room. But of course these are not there for the purpose of relaxation, but rather to offer the opportunity of sitting while one is engaged in light and stimulating conversation. It is easier to chat while seated on a small, capricious chair than on a high-backed armchair. It is for this reason that such chairs are built in England; they were on view last year at the Scala Christmas Exhibition at the Austrian Museum. The Viennese, either because they did not know what the chairs were to be used for or perhaps because they had in mind a patented chair for all possible sitting eventualities, called them impractical.

In any case one ought to use the term "impractical" very advisedly. I have already made the point earlier that in certain circumstances even an uncomfortable position may be considered comfortable. The Greeks, who demanded from a seat that it allow the backbone plenty of room for movement, would doubtless find our backrests very uncomfortable since we require that our shoulder blades be supported. And what would they think of the American rocking chair, of which we still do not know how to make head or tail! For we go on the principle that one must rock when sitting on a rocking chair. But I am convinced that this incorrect assumption is the result of its incorrect name. In America the chair is called a "rocker." The word "rocking" signifies, however, a gentle swaying movement back and forth. The rocker is in principle nothing but a chair with two legs, such that the feet of the person who is seated in it must act as the two front legs. It developed from the comfortable sitting position that one attains when his center of gravity is shifted to the rear and his front legs are elevated. The back runners of the chair prevent it from tipping over backward. The American rocker does not have front runners like our rocking chairs because it would never occur to any individual to rock himself. It is for this reason that one finds only rockers in so many American rooms, while here they are still downright unpopular.

Thus every chair should be practical. If we would only make practical chairs for people, we would give them the possibility of furnishing their homes completely without the aid of the interior decorator. Perfect furniture makes perfect rooms. Once it becomes a matter of living space rather than showy rooms, our upholsterers, architects, painters, sculptors, interior decorators, and so on ought to restrict themselves to producing perfect and practical furniture. At present we are dependent on English imports to fulfill this need; unfortunately there is no better advice to be given to our carpenters than to copy the English models. Certainly our carpenters might have produced similar chairs without any influence at all if they had not been cut off from contact with life. For there are such small differences between pieces of furniture made by carpenters at *one* cultural period and at *one and the same* time that only the expert can spot them.

It seems quite comical that at the waning of our century voices can be heard peremptorily demanding emancipation from the English influence in favor of an Austrian national style. Applied to the design of the bicycle, this demand would sound something like this: "Give up the degenerate copying of articles manufactured in England! Take as your model instead the authentically Austrian modern wheel by the Upper Styrian farmhand Peter Zapfel! This wheel is better suited to Alpine landscape than the ugly English wheel."

From century to century furniture has taken on more and more kindred traits. Even at the beginning of the century it was difficult to tell the difference between a chair made in Vienna and one made in London. That was at a time when it took weeks of riding in a post chaise to cover the distance between Vienna and London. But now there are strange fellows who in this era of express trains and telegraphs want to build a second Great Wall of China around us. But it is impossible. Similar eating results in similar silverware; similar work and similar relaxation will have the same chair as their consequence. It would be an offense against our culture if it were to be demanded of us that we give up our customary methods of eating and instead eat out of one bowl like the peasant and his family, simply because our way of eating originated in England. And it is the same for sitting. Our customs are much closer to those of the English than to those of the Upper Austrian peasant.

Our carpenters would have thus arrived at the same results if they had simply been left alone and the architects had not mixed in. If the converging of the forms had continued at the same pace as was maintained from the Renaissance up to the time of the Congress of Vienna, then there would be almost no difference now between the carpentry in all the different nations, just as there is none in those flourishing crafts in which the architects have played no part: the building of carriages, jewelry making, fancy leather work. For there is no difference between the mentality of a London carpenter and that of his Viennese counterpart. But there is a world of difference between the mentality of the London carpenter and that of the Viennese architect.

24 Boston rocker, c. 1840.

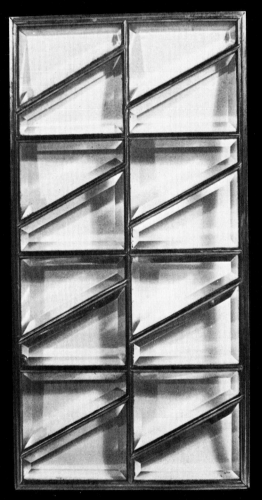

25 *Crystal and brass window,*
attributed to Adolf Loos, c. 1900.
26 *Situla. From Gottfried Semper,*
Der Stil in den Technischen und
Tektonischen Künsten, oder
Praktische Aesthetik, *Munich, 1879.*
27 *Hydria. From Gottfried Semper,*
Der Stil...

"By looking at the pots that a certain people produced, we are able to tell in a general way what kind of race they were and how advanced their civilization was." So says Semper in the foreword to his "Pottery."* One might add that it is not only pots that are informed with this revelatory power. Every implement can tell something about the customs and character of a people. But pottery artifacts do so most palpably.

Semper immediately gives us an example. He describes the vessel which women in Egypt used to bring water to the house and that which Greek women used for the same purpose. The former is called the "Nile pail" or "situla"; it is a container that looks very much like those copper basins with which the Venetians draw their water. Similar to a giant gourd that has been cut open at the top, it has no feet and a handle like a fire bucket. This pail for drawing water can reveal to us a whole land formation, its topography, its water systems. We know the following immediately: the people who used this vessel must have lived on a low-lying plain, on the banks of a slow-moving river. How different the Greek vessel is! Semper says this about it:

" . . . The hydria's function is not to draw water, but rather to catch it as it flows from the spring. Hence the funnel form of the neck and the basin form of the body, whose center of gravity is located as near as possible to the mouth of the vessel. The Etruscan and Greek woman carried the hydria on her head, upright when it was full and horizontally when empty. Whoever has tried to balance a cane on the end of his finger will have discovered that the trick is most easily performed if he places the heaviest end of the cane on top. This experiment explains the basic form of the Greek hydria (the body actually resembles a heart-shaped beet), whose final perfection derives from two horizontal handles at the level of the center of gravity with which to pick up the vessel when full, and a third, vertical handle for carrying and hanging up the vessel when empty. This third handle might perhaps also have served as a grip for a third person, who would help the woman who was to bear the water to lift the full vessel onto her head."

That's Semper. He probably cut many an idealist to the quick with his words. How could Semper attribute these magnificent Greek vases, with their perfect forms that seem created solely to tell of the Greek people's desire for beauty, merely to necessity? The feet, the body, the handles, the size of the mouth dictated only by function? But that would mean that these vases are ultimately just *practical!* And we always thought they were *beautiful!* But how could that be? For we have always been taught: practicality excludes beauty.

In my last article I ventured to assert the opposite. Subsequently I have received so many letters demonstrating to me that I am wrong that I must take refuge behind the ancient Greeks. I do not want to deny that our arts and crafts industry is of such a high standing that it completely precludes any comparison with other peoples or epochs. But I would like to think that the ancient Greeks also understood a little bit about beauty. And so they created only that which was practical, without concerning themselves in the least with that which was beautiful, without worrying about complying with an aesthetic imperative. When an object was made so practical that it could not be made any more practical, then they called it beautiful. Subsequent peoples called it beautiful as well, and we too say: these vases are beautiful.

Are there still people today who work as the Greeks worked? Yes indeed! The English do so as a nation, the engineers as a profession. The English and the engineers are our Greeks. It is from them that we acquire our culture; from them

Glass and Clay

Neue Freie Presse, *June 26, 1898*

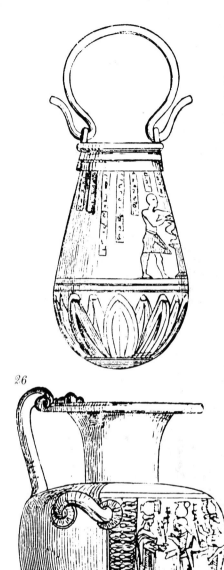

26

27

*Gottfried Semper, *Der stil [in den technischen und tektonischen künsten, oder praktische aesthetik* (Munich, 1879)].

that it spreads over the entire globe. They are the consummate men of the nineteenth century . . .

The Greek vases are beautiful, as beautiful as a machine, as beautiful as a bicycle. In this regard, our pottery cannot compete with the products of the engineering industry. That is as seen, of course, not from the Viennese point of view, but from the Greek one. At the beginning of the century our pottery was entirely absorbed in the classical element. Here too the architect felt obliged to come to the "rescue."

I once went to an operetta the action of which took place in Spain. Some sort of joyful festivity was being depicted—I think the head of the household was celebrating his birthday—and a chorus of students was called for; in this way, an opportunity was provided for the composer to create a Spanish song and for the costumer to make a certain number of outfits for male roles. These students sing the same song over and over again, whatever the occasion—wedding, birthday, baptism, jubilee, or name day:
We have just a single song,
We sing it in all cases,
So now, singers, to your places!

This magical song goes as follows:
To your health, to your health, to your health!

I am citing the lines imprecisely from memory, as I saw the production at least ten years ago.

Our architects were like these students. They knew only one song. It had two verses: the profile and the ornament. And everything was fashioned and worked with the same profile and the same ornament—facades and wallets, inkwells and pianos, key boards and exhibition designs. Glass and pottery objects, too. First the artist drew a line, and then to the left or to the right of it, depending on whether he was right- or left-handed, he began to draw profiles, and more profiles. It was a joy to behold it. The profiles seemed to flow freely out of the pen. A flat bit, a rounded bit, a flat bit, a bump, a flat bit, a rounded bit, a flat bit, a bump, and in between, a molding every now and then. Then this profile was traced over again, and the rotational figure was finished. Now came the second verse: the ornament. This too was solved with the help of geometry, not in order to relate it to the specific meaning of the thing, as the song makes clear, but rather to allow the rotational figure to be generated. In short, the results were splendid.

Then came the evil English and spoiled the pleasure of the men at the drawing board. They said, Do not draw! Produce! Go out into the world so that you will know what is needed. And when you have understood life, only then take your place before the forge and the potter's wheel. As a result, ninety-nine percent of the artists gave up pottery making.

Here, of course, we have not yet come so far. But the English mentality has already reached our craftsmen and is making them rebel against the domination of architecture. I was secretly delighted to hear recently the complaint of a colleague of mine that a potter to whom he had given a drawing had refused outright to follow it. He did not even want to make the attempt. He simply did not want to be "rescued." "The man was right," I told the architect. The latter probably thought I was crazy.

It is high time that our crafts begin to think of themselves and attempt to shake off all unasked-for domination. Whoever wants to contribute, let him be welcome. Whoever wants to work at the humming potter's wheel in his potter's apron alongside the others or with a naked chest in front of the glowing furnace, let him be praised. But as for those dilettantes who from their comfortable studios want to prescribe and trace out for the artist (art comes from know-how), for the man who produces, just what he should do, let them keep to their *own* field—that of graphic art.

The emancipation of the craftsman began in England, and it is for this reason that all of the new objects have English forms. The new cut glass that we call *steindl* cut or *walzen* cut originated in England. Lines through the prism's cross-section form a geometric decoration over the whole glass. The straight-edge ornament is called by the first name, the round-edge ornament by the second. This technique of cutting has reached such a high level that we are already capable of competing with America (a country where the technique has reached full bloom), which should cause no surprise given the skill of our glass cutters. Many of our pieces are more delicate, more elegant, and more sophisticated in form. The American cut glass is characterized by an exuberance of form that in my opinion seems inappropriate to the times. Nearly all the exhibitors provide good examples of their work.

One now sees Tiffany glasses manufactured on Austrian soil for the first time. The son of the American goldsmith Tiffany, Louis C. Tiffany, has invented a new method of glass decoration; it was made possible by the newest advances in liquid glass technology, which he developed with the help of Venetian glass workers. The technique does not depend on cutting or painting, but rather on the artistic dipping of the piece into vats of multicolored glass, so that unlike the Venetian method, which welds different pieces together during the blowing, the Tiffany method fashions the vessel's shape out of one piece during the blowing. The form created is probably the most advanced that modern craftsmanship is able to offer. The Neuwelt[1] objects are quite tame, especially in their coloration. But it is a beginning all the same.

We cannot speak of the pottery industry with the same confidence. Porcelain painting still holds fast to the overly precious and pretty tradition of the last century. There are forms, forms to be made in earthenware and majolica! Among other things we find an ashtray composed of the concave arms of the imperial house. Is there no bureau of heraldry that can do something about this? There is assuredly much that is inferior in the glassware too. One passes over it in silence. But in the pottery section there hangs this self-assured sign: "All designs and forms are protected by law in all countries." Good God! Shouldn't one instead legally protect all countries against these designs and forms? This thought must occur to many when they see such tastelessness thrusting itself to the fore.

At the large exhibition of the firm of Wahliss appear sample dishes from the major table services already produced. These have delighted all. In this field, that firm has made an unrivaled place for itself around the world. All the royal houses and the aristocracy both by birth and by money from all parts of the world have their porcelain services manufactured here. The plates for the Indian rajah and for an American Croesus stand side by side. These dishes seem to me a symbol of the beginning of an era in which *one* culture will prevail in the entire world.

29 Pottery urn manufactured by Ernst Wahliss, exhibited at the Winter Exhibition, Austrian Museum for Art and Industry, Vienna. From Kunst und Kunsthandwerk, *no. 2, 1899.*

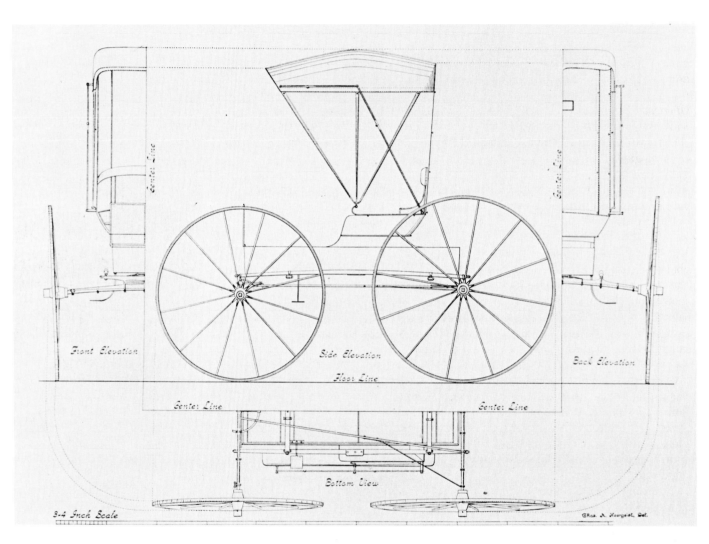

30 American one-man buggy. From
The Carriage Monthly, *vol. 32,*
Philadelphia, October 1896.

"Neustadt! All off!" Several people get off. "But we want to go to Steffelsdorf." "Well then, you have to take the post chaise for another two hours." "What? Be tossed around for two more hours? That's appalling." We are in Austria.

"Kingston! All off!" Several people get off here too. But they want to go to Longsdale. "Well then, you have to take the post chaise for another two hours." "What? The post chaise? How delightful . . ." We are in England.

We Austrians think to ourselves that these must be strange folk who at the end of the nineteenth century would prefer to be tossed around in a mail coach rather than ride in a comfortable train car. But let us think about ourselves for a moment. We would rather ride in a fiacre than in a steam train or an electric streetcar. Of course, only in those situations when we will be observed. For without a gaping audience, even the quickest little carriage is no fun. Let's be honest and admit it calmly.

Of course, just driving itself is enough to delight the English. In their hearts and souls they still have the poetry of the country road. When the Englishman is in the city, it is only in an emergency that he will take a cab or a hansom. Even the most elegant lady takes her place on the omnibus or the tram and is pleased to get a place on the Imperial in the summertime. In our country we creep ashamed into the very back of the car and are thoroughly wretched when an acquaintance catches us on the bus. If one is going out to the country, however, then one takes one's place in the train together with everyone else.

But in England when someone goes to the country, he takes a seat in the post chaise, the mail coach. He sits not in a narrow coupé, not in a landau, but high on the roof of the coach, with men, women, children, everything colorfully confused, four fresh horses in front, while the guard—the conductor—blows a merry tune on his long horn. No one above sits sluggish and bored, leaning back in his seat as if to say to the passersby, "Come on, look at me!" Instead they laugh, have a good time, are merry and full of good cheer. One big family.

Everyone in England can afford to indulge in this pleasure. The great demand has made it less expensive. The coach leaves from every large hotel at an appointed hour. One drives far, far into the country where there are no more onlookers. It seems, of course, from the Viennese point of view, to be a frivolous pleasure. But whoever is wealthy and owns horses also owns his own coach. Of course, it is not a real mail coach anymore, but rather a private version of one, which is called a "drag." Friends are often invited to a coaching party. One of the two grooms blows the horn, and the citizens of the suburbs throw open their windows and hum along with lively postilion tunes.

The whole thing is so well suited to the character of the English people, to their profound love of nature. No one abhors machines more than the Englishman. Wherever he can free himself from them he does so. Machines belong to the work world; he tries to keep them far away from his private life. He is the most susceptible of all to the call of the countryside's poetry. One has to have lived in England to be able to understand this sentence that I once read in a newspaper article: "Today the English nobility still prefer to travel in a mail coach; they have their servants travel by train."

It is possible that we too may progress this far some day. Many people think that it would be unfortunate if we were to give up something national and replace it

The Luxury Vehicle

Neue Freie Presse, *July 3, 1898*

31 Omnibus. From Franz Merklein, Praktisches Handbuch für den Gesammten Wagenbau, *Atlas, Vienna, Pest, and Leipzig, 1896.*

with something English. I do not think so. In the last century we believed that the plains were beautiful and the mountains abhorrent. Has it hurt us that we have left behind this childish fear of the mountains and taken over from the English the love for the high ranges? But the English meant to have not just a platonic relationship with the mountains. They did not remain down in the valley staring up at the soaring pinnacles, but climbed up them, in spite of the head-shaking of the Germans, who were astounded at the "crazy" English. And today? Have we not all become English?

If we have convinced ourselves of the poetry of the mountains, we will probably soon enjoy the beauty of the country road as well. Our carriage industry is ready.* It has been on a par with the English for quite a time now. There is no need for our manufacturers to do themselves even the slightest violence. What they find beautiful is considered beautiful by the English coachbuilder as well, so that it is difficult to discover any significant differences between the English and the Viennese coaches. The Englishman and the man from Vienna have only one ambition: to build elegant coaches. And both come up with the same results.

*The automobile did not yet exist at that time. But it is here anticipated. The first sections of this essay may serve to demonstrate that an object must first exist in the imagination before it is invented. *1931*.

He who is a true German arts and crafts worker will take issue strongly with these results. "One again sees here," the man will figure, "that the English have no taste. And the Viennese do not have any either." He will think melancholy thoughts about the elegant state coaches of the seventeenth and eighteenth centuries, their glistening splendor, their rich decoration, and their shiny gilding. Yes, if only such a manufacturer would call on him. But no, even the most taste-less junk pleases these people and their customers. That is how the old-timer thinks. But the young craftsman, with his head full of ornaments on paper (he calls the paper his "studio"), would most dearly like to give the coach a "modern" decor and set ornament loose on the unfortunate vehicle.

But the coachbuilder says to both of them, "Just what is the matter with you? The coach is fine as it is." "But it has no ornament." Both show him their designs. The coachbuilder laughs and replies, "I really like my own coach better." "Well, tell us why!" "Because it has no ornament."

Because it has no ornament! How the coachbuilder towers over the man of arts and crafts, whether architect, painter, or upholsterer. Let us briefly review a few chapters of the history of civilization. The lower the cultural level of a people, the more extravagant it is with its ornament, its decoration. The Indian covers every object, every boat, every oar, every arrow with layer upon layer of ornament. To see decoration as a sign of superiority means to stand at the level of the Indians. But we must overcome the Indian in us. The Indian says, "This woman is beautiful because she wears gold rings in her nose and ears." The man of high culture says, "This woman is beautiful because she does not wear rings in her nose and ears." To seek beauty only in form and not in ornament is the goal toward which all humanity is striving.**

**The first battle cry against ornament. *1931*.

Our coachbuilding industry, like our leather fancy-goods and luggage industries, must attribute its superiority solely to the happy circumstance that no professional school for coachbuilding has been established. For in all the professional schools the crafts are reduced to the level of the Indians. But in fact one branch of the coach industry had great need, and still has, of a professional school. The architect could not have spoiled anything here, because they would have had no use for him. I am speaking of the heavy vehicle industry.

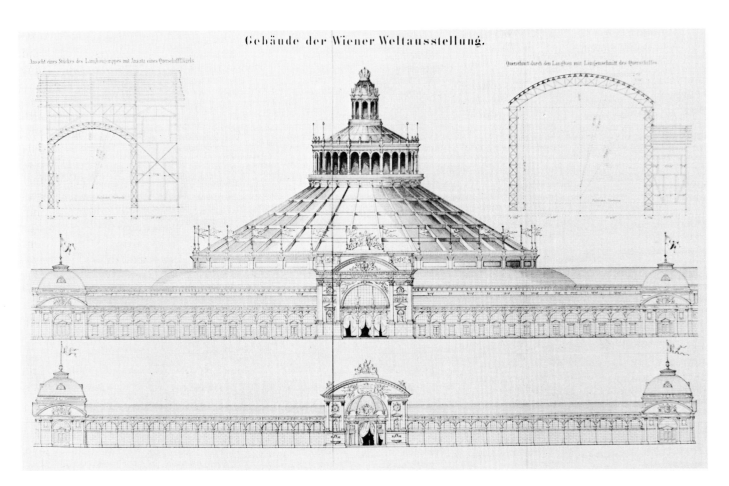

Gebäude der Wiener Weltausstellung.

32 *Elevation and structural details of the Rotunda. This exhibition building was designed for the Vienna World's Fair of 1873 after a sketch by the English architect Scott Russel, and executed by Austrian architects under R. von Engerth, Vienna, 1872-1873. From* Zeitschrift für Architekten- und Ingenieurwesen zu Hannover, *Hanover, 1873.*

The heavy vehicle industry in other countries has reached a level which our own has not even approached. Unfortunately our contractors were not required to be concerned about improvements. All improvements and modifications were dictated by one desire only: to reduce the number of workers necessary to load and unload. But in Austria the cost of human labor is still so low that there is no cause for concern about such things. If a stone of four cubic meters has to be picked up, there are at least twenty men involved in the task. The same maneuver is carried out in unloading it. The cost is "not worth mentioning." But it is different in America. There the driver pulls up, makes a slight movement with his hand which does not tax him in the least and which lasts at most three minutes, and then drives away. And the stone? It is already in the cart. It is unloaded in just the same way. The whole secret of this procedure lies in the ingenious construction of the cart. The stone is transported not in the cart but underneath it, suspended approximately thirty centimeters above the ground. The driver pulls up over the stone that is to be loaded, raises it a little bit to slip chains under it, and then turns a crank, which lifts the stone. And thus for everything, for coal and for the plate glass used in large display windows, a special cart is built. Here a school might help us break with the old, worn-out methods. We need such a school the way one needs a morsel of bread—therefore we will probably have to wait a pretty long time for it.

The luxury vehicle has undergone a remarkable revolution in recent years. Here too Vienna threatens to lag behind. It has to do with the great popularity that the C-spring has won. The reader will remember that the normal carriage possesses springs comprised of two segments of a circle which meet to form two angles. These are called compression springs. More elegant carriages have additional springs that are curved like a C. The boot of the coach is set between these, hanging on straps. This kind of carriage, the carriage with eight springs, or to use the technical term, the carriage *à huit ressorts*, has exclusively come to dominate vehicles for every kind of city excursion in all the great metropolises of the world in which it is represented. Only Vienna lags behind. It is not as if our carriage builders are unable to build this kind of carriage. It is just that the contracts are lacking. The reason for this remarkable circumstance may be found in the fact that the Chief Bureau for Court Affairs has not yet introduced this type of carriage. Our carriage industry waits with yearning. Our court is in fact the only one that today still does not use the carriage *à huit ressorts*. Stately people must still ride in a coupé which, with a different coat of paint and modified accessories (upholstery), might well be seen on line at a taxi stand.

Our carriage industry has represented itself magnificently in the Rotunda. There is absolutely nothing inferior to be seen; it is perhaps the only industry of which this can be said. Armbruster has displayed two interesting carriages of the British type of the fifties and sixties—this conservatism is evidence of the eminence of the firm. They also have exhibited a drag which is totally correct down to the last detail. Lohner has a mail coach on display. It is interesting to test our carriages for their correctness against the regulations that the London Coaching Club has established for these two types. This club sponsors two meetings each year. In London these are always treated as national festivals. Only those drags and coaches are admitted which correspond to the rules. The deviations of our carriages are naturally not a burden to the manufacturers, but to those who place the orders, since of course no one will intentionally manufacture an incorrect carriage.

On Armbruster's drag, the one with the black boot, yellow chassis and wheels,

33

34

35

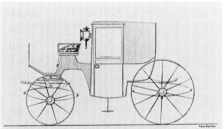

36

37

and dark blue incised lines, the placement of the coat of arms is very distracting. It belongs on the lower part of the carriage door, and should really be significantly larger. Inside, the hat straps, the pockets on the doors, and the hooks on which to hang the lanterns are missing. For during the day the lanterns must be stored inside the carriage. As for the rear seats—take a look at the backrests and compare them with those on Lohner's coach; the reserve bar[1] should hang over the splinter bars.[2] This backrest is in fact the most prominent feature of a drag. But here the seat is only dimensioned for two grooms and for this reason has no backrest; this is in contrast to the coach, where the back seat must allow for two additional guests and the guard.

The hinges for the rear trunk are misplaced on the coach. They should be located on the right side and not underneath, as on the drag, where the open trunk door has to serve as a table. The strap net[3] between the two middle seats is correct on the coach, however, while it should not appear in the drag. The backrests should be so constructed that they do not flap over. On the drag this is permitted. Thus we see that these two vehicles have overstepped the guidelines that the Coaching Club established. In their color, however, they are both correct.

The Nesseldorfer Society has represented itself especially well with its charabanc hunting coach of light wood and pigskin. A charming effect. J. Weigl exhibits an American buggy that is so well done that one would be hard put to find as perfect a one even in its own native land. But in general I would like to caution against the most recent "advances" of the American carriage-building industry. Technically they are certainly unrivaled. But there are often mistakes in the form. For example, they are now beginning over there to adorn their carriages with unfortunate acanthus leaves. That's the Indian in them.

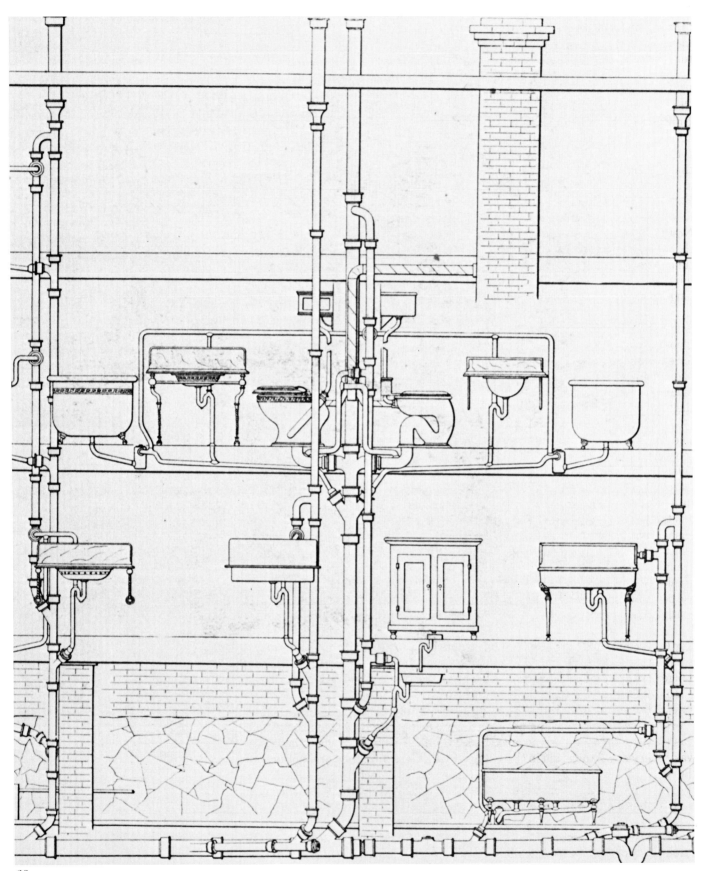

It would be quite easy to imagine our century without carpenters; we would simply use iron furniture.* We could just as well do without the stonemason; the cement worker would take over his work. But there would be no nineteenth century without the plumber. He has left his mark and become indispensable to us.

We think that we have to give him a French name. We call him the *installateur*. This is wrong. For this man is the pillar of the Germanic idea of culture. The English were the keepers and protectors of this culture and therefore deserve to take precedence when we are looking around for a name for this man. Besides, the word "plumber" comes from the Latin—*plumbum* means "lead"—and is thus for the English as well as for us not a foreign word, but a borrowed word.

For a century and a half now we have been receiving our culture secondhand: from the French. We have never rebelled against the leadership of the French. Now that we realize that we have been duped by the French, now that we realize that the English have been leading the French around by the nose for a long time, we are setting up a front of German culture against the English. We did not mind being guided by the French; it was very pleasant. But the thought that the English are really the leaders—that makes us nervous.

And yet Germanic culture has extended its victorious campaign over the entire globe. Whoever cooperates with it becomes great and powerful: the Japanese, for example. Whoever takes a stand against it remains backward: the Chinese. We must accept Germanic culture despite the fact that we Germans still very much resist it. It does us no good at all, even when we raise a hue and cry against the "English disease."[1] Our prospects for life, our very existence depend on it.

The English have remained somewhat apart from the great hustle and bustle of the world. And as the Icelandic people have preserved the Germanic myth for us down through the centuries, so too the Roman waves that broke upon the English coast and the cliffs of Scotland washed away the last traces of a Germanic culture from the German soil. For the Germans had become Romanized in feeling and thought. But now they are reacquiring their own culture back from the English. And as the German always holds on with his well-known tenacity to that which he has once obtained, he now struggles against English culture because it seems new to him. Even Lessing had quite a time trying to make the great Germanic mode of thinking accessible to the Germans. Step by step one stand after the other had to be made against the various Gottscheds[2] who arose. And just recently the same battle raged in the studios of the carpenters.

Our Gottscheds and with them all the imitators of French culture and manners are fighting a losing battle. We no longer fear the mountains or shy away from danger; we no longer flee the dust of the road, the smell of the forest, or fatigue. Gone is our fear of getting dirty, our solemn awe of water. When the Roman view of the world still prevailed, around the time of the great Ludwig,[3] no one ever got dirty, but of course no one ever washed either. Only common people washed. The upper class was enameled. "He must be quite a slob if he has to wash every day," they said in those days . . . In Germany, they probably speak the same way today. I read this answer as a matter of fact just recently in the *fliegende*.[4] It was a father's response to his young son who relayed the message from his teacher that he should wash daily.

The Englishman is unacquainted with the fear of getting dirty. He goes into the stable, strokes his horse, mounts it, and takes off across the wide heath. The

Plumbers

Neue Freie Presse, *July 17, 1898*

*Here the first impulse arises for steel furniture. Today it has become modern. *1931*.

38 "Complete plumbing of a new residence. An up-to-date piece of work in Hartford, Connecticut, by R. M. Starbuck." From The Plumbers' Journal: Gas, Steam, and Hot Water Fitters' Review, *vol. 27, Chicago, 1900.*

Englishman does everything himself; he hunts, he climbs mountains, and he saws up trees. He gets no pleasure out of being a spectator. Germanic knighthood has found a refuge on the English isle and from there has conquered the world again. Between Maximilian, the last knight, and our epoch there lies the long period of the Roman occupation. Charles VI on the Martinswand![5] Unthinkable! Full wig and Alpine air! Charles VI would never have been allowed to climb to the top of the mountains like a simple hunter! He would have had to be carried up in a sedan chair—if, that is, he had ever even expressed what would have been a strange desire for the times.

In such times the plumbers had nothing to do and this is how they lost their name. Of course there were water supply systems, water for fountains, water for looking at. But baths, showers, and water closets were not provided. Water for washing was very sparingly rationed. In the German villages that preserve the Roman culture, you can still today find washbasins that we Anglicized city dwellers wouldn't know how to begin to use. It was not always like this. Germany was famous for its water use in the Middle Ages. The great public baths (of which the so-called *bader*, the barber, is the sole vestige today) were always crowded, and everyone took at least one bath a day. Although there are generally no baths to be found in the later royal palaces, in the house of the German burgher the bathroom was the most splendid and sumptuous room. Who has not heard of the famous bathrooms in the Fugger house in Augsburg,[6] that crowning jewel of the German Renaissance! When the German view of the world was standard, it wasn't only Germans who indulged in sport, amusement, and hunting.

We have remained backward. Some time ago I asked an American lady what seemed to her the most noticeable difference between Austria and America. Her answer: the plumbing! The sanitary installations, heating, lighting, and water supply systems. Our taps, sinks, water closets, washstands, and other things are still far inferior to the English and American fittings. What must seem most remarkable to an American is that in order to wash our hands, we must first go down the hall for a jug of water since there are toilets that do not have washing facilities. In this respect, America is to Austria as Austria is to China. It will be objected that we too already have such accommodations. Certainly, but not everywhere. Even in China there is English plumbing, for the wealthy and for foreigners. But the majority of people haven't heard of it.

A home without a room for bathing! Impossible in America. The thought that at the end of the nineteenth century there is still a nation with a population of millions whose inhabitants cannot bathe daily seems atrocious to an American. Thus even in the poorest sections of New York it is possible to find dormitory accommodations for ten cents which are cleaner and more pleasant than our village inns. This is why there is only a single waiting room for all classes in America, since even in the largest crowd the slightest odor is not noticeable.

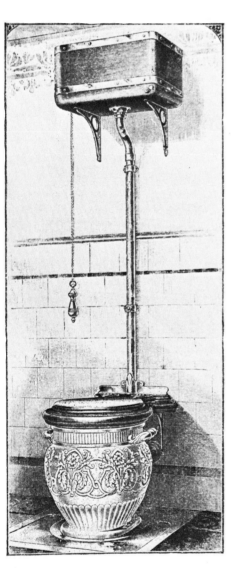

39 "Grecian vase toilet" manufactured by J. L. Mott Iron Works, New York. From William Paul Gerhard, Entwasserungs-Anlagen Amerikanischer Gebäude. Fortschritte auf dem Gebiete der Architektur: Erganzungshefte zum Handbuch der Architektur, *no. 10, Stuttgart, 1897.*

In the thirties, one of the members of "Young Germany"[7]—it was Laube in the *krieger*—made a great statement: Germany needs a good bath. But let's consider this seriously. We really do not need art at all. We do not even have a culture yet. Here is where the state might come to the rescue. Instead of putting the cart before the horse, instead of spending their money on the production of art, they should first try to produce a culture. Next to the academies we should build baths, and along with the professors we should appoint bath attendants. A higher standard of culture will have better art as its consequence, an art that, when it comes to the fore, will do so without the help of the state.

46

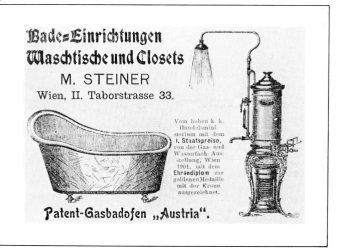
40

41

42

40 Advertisement by the firm of Carl Becker & Franz Both for a "rocking wave bath." From Neue Freie Presse, *Vienna, August 28, 1898.*

41 Advertisement by the firm of Carl Becker & Franz Both for a "steambath apparatus." From Neue Freie Presse, *September 25, 1898.*

42 Advertisement by the firm of M. Steiner for bathtubs and overhead showers. From Wiener Bauindustrie-Zeitung, *no. 32, 1902.*

43

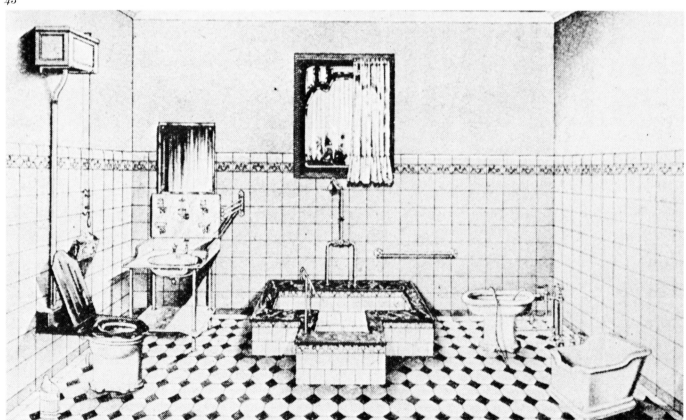

44

But the German—I am thinking only of the great majority—uses too little water for his body and in his home. He only uses water when he has to, when someone tells him that it is good for his health. A clever peasant in Silesia[8] and a clever priest in the Bavarian mountains[9] each prescribed water as a medicament. It helped. People with the most severe hydrophobia splashed about in the water. And they were cured too. This is perfectly natural. Who does not know the story of the Eskimo who complained to a traveler of an old chest ailment? The traveler put a plaster on his chest and promised the disbelieving patient that he would be healed by the following day. The plaster was removed, and the pains had disappeared along with a thick layer of dirt that clung to the bandage. A miracle cure! It is sad that many people can only be moved to clean, wash, and bathe by such means. If the need existed generally, the state would have to reckon with it. And if every bedroom did not have its own bath, the state would have to build huge baths next to which the Thermae of Caracalla would look like a powder room. The state does have a certain interest in increasing the desire for cleanliness in its people. For only *that* people which approaches the English in water use can keep step with them economically; only *that* people which surpasses the English in water use water is destined to wrest from them the sovereignty of the world.

But the plumber is the pioneer of cleanliness. He is the state's chief craftsman, the quartermaster of culture, that is, of today's prevailing culture. Every English washbasin with its spigot and drain is a marvel of progress. Every stove with its fittings for frying and roasting meat over an open flame is a new victory of the German spirit. Such a revolution is also apparent on Viennese menus. The consumption of roast beef, grilled steaks, and cutlets increases constantly, while that of wiener schnitzel and roast chicken (those Italian dishes), as well as of stewed, boiled, and steamed French specialties constantly decreases.

Our bathroom fittings might well be our weakest point. Instead of covering the bathtub with white tiles, people in this country would rather use colored tiles so that—as one manufacturer naively assured me (he is not in the exhibition)—the dirt will be less visible. Tin tubs too are enameled in dark colors instead of in white, the only suitable color. Finally, there are tin bathtubs that aim to look as if they are marble. And there are people who believe it, since these marbleized tubs also find their purchasers. Even those good folk who still see things from the Indian point of view (as everyone knows, the Indian decorated everything he could lay his hands on) are well provided for. There are Rococo flush valves, Rococo taps, even Rococo washstands. It is truly lucky that a few firms also undertake to provide for the non-Indians. Thus at M. Steiner's we see excellent American-style overhead showers, a new invention, all smooth and thus very elegant. H. Esders produces fixtures that are efficient and correct in both form and color. It is still worth mentioning from a purely technical point of view that the continued use of the crank valve in plumbing, in the age of the rotary valve, can no longer be justified. It is old hat, an old hat that ought to be thrown away. The crank valve is no less expensive, but wears out more quickly, and gives rise to many other inconveniences. Even if our plumbers do not want it, the public should work in its own interest and insist on the adoption of the rotary valve.

An increase in the use of water is one of our most critical cultural tasks. May our Viennese plumbers fulfill their task and bring us closer to that most important goal, the attainment of a cultural level equal to the rest of the civilized Western world. For otherwise, something very unpleasant, very shameful could happen to us. Otherwise, if both nations continue to progress at their present rate, the Japanese could attain Germanic culture before the Austrians do.

45

43 *An English bathroom of 1901 as advertised in the W. E. Mason Catalogue.*
44 *A Viennese bathroom from an advertisement for Rudolf Ditmar's Decorative Tile Factory in Vienna. From* Das Interieur IV, *1903.*
45 *Vincenz Priessnitz's water therapy. From Philo vom Walde [Johannes Reinelt],* Vincenz Priessnitz: Sein Leben und Sein Wirken, *Berlin, 1898.*

How is fashion determined? Who determines fashion? These are clearly very difficult questions.

Neue Freie Presse, *July 24, 1898*

The Vienna Hatters Association reserved the right to solve these problems in a playful manner, at least in the area of headgear. It meets twice a year around an official green table and dictates to the whole world exactly what model of hat will be worn in the following season. To the whole world, mind you. It will not be a hat that belongs to the Viennese local costume; it will not be a hat that our firemen, cabbies, idlers, dandies, and other Viennese local types will make use of. Oh no, the members of the Hatters Association do not worry their heads about these people. For hat fashion is intended strictly for the gentleman, and everyone knows that the clothing of the gentleman has nothing in common with the sundry apparel of the masses—except, of course, in the area of athletics, which is, as we know, an earthier activity. And as gentlemen all over the world dress alike, the Vienna Hatters Association sets the style for headgear throughout the entire Western cultural world.

Who would have thought that the solution to these questions could be so simple! One may look at the honest master hatter now with respect. He cast his vote for a further increase in the height of the silk hat and thus joined in with the majority. Thus he alone forced the loiterers from Paris to Yokohama to wear a higher silk hat the following year if they wished to be counted among polite society. But what do the loiterers from Paris to Yokohama know, what do they guess of the honest master who works somewhere in the Eleventh District! They talk a lot of twaddle about the tyranny of fashion, perhaps, or in a more positive moment, of the moody goddess of fashion! If they would suspect that the good hatter of the Eleventh District is the tyrant, the god!

46 Ita hat factory showroom, the Graben, Vienna. From Das Interieur I, *1900.*

The consequences would be unthinkable if this man had been prevented from appearing at the hat fashion elections—whether because of a head cold, or because her ladyship his wife had not left him free on that evening, or because he had totally forgotten. Then the world would have had to wear a lower top hat. Therefore one must hope that the members of the Hatters Association, in the face of their colossal responsibility, let nothing prevent them from casting their vote two times a year.

I seem to hear my readers posing this question: yes, but do the hatters in Paris and London, in New York and Bombay allow the fashion to be set by the Viennese masters? I must answer dejectedly, unfortunately not. These awful men, with perfidious Albion at their head, of course, do not even trouble themselves to find out the results of the vote. So are these votes in Vienna really quite pointless? Actually—yes. These votes are a harmless game, just as harmless as they would be if cast by the hatters of Bucharest or the hatters of Chicago. The kind of hat that fashionable gentlemen wear, gentlemen who will be considered fashionable everywhere in the world, is not even touched by these votes.

But wait a minute, this game is not quite so harmless after all. There are actually more fashionable people than our hatters usually assume. And since these people will not wear hats whose fashionableness ceases to exist beyond the black and yellow frontier signs at the border, and since, however, our hatters on the recommendation of the Association only produce such hats, the people of fashion are forced to purchase hats made in England. And we see how the consumption of English hats in Austria, even though the same quality hat is almost a hundred percent more expensive, increases by this same percentage from year to year, while the type of hat recommended by the Association becomes increasingly remote from that worn by those who dominate the fashion world. This fact is all the sadder when one thinks that because our felt is of such excellent quality and offered at such inexpensive prices, we could easily be competitive with the whole world. But the importation of the Viennese hat abroad founders constantly because of its incorrect form and construction.

Our leading firms have had the worst experience with their fashionable customers because of the models recommended by the Hatters Association, and they have quickly given up following their standards. One will not be able to find such forms at Pless's or Habig's. This emancipation soon became noticeable on the export market. Habig hats can be purchased all over the globe, in New York as well as in Rio de Janeiro. But I do not understand why the court hatter, who can procure the correct kind of hats thanks to his foreign connections and his fashionable circle of customers, should carry a different kind of hat from the master in the provinces.

The Hatters Association has only to publicize that form of hat which is accepted as modern all over the world, and especially in the very best circles, rather than passing off as modern a hat created by the whim of one of its members. As a consequence, exports would increase and imports would decrease. Finally, it would also be no misfortune if everyone, down to the man in the smallest provincial town, would wear just as elegant a hat as the Viennese aristocrat. The times of dress code regulations are really over. But many of the decisions of this Association have a direct negative effect on our hat industry. The top hat will now be worn somewhat lower than last season. The Association, however, has decided that next season's top hat should be heightened once again. And the result of this? The English hatters are already preparing now for an extraordinary volume of exports of silk hats to the Austrian market since modern top hats will not be able to be had from the Viennese hatmakers next winter.

The activity of the Association could also be aimed in another direction to good effect. The national hat of Austria, the loden hat, is beginning to make its tour of the world. It has already appeared in England. The Prince of Wales encountered it on his hunting trips in Austria, became enamored of it, and took the style home with him. Thus the loden hat, for men as well as for women, has conquered English society. It is truly a critical moment, especially for the loden hat industry. The question is, of course, who is going to make the loden hats for English society? The Austrians, of course—so long as the Austrians produce those styles that English society desires. But an infinite amount of sensitivity is necessary for this, an exact knowledge of society, a feeling for elegance and a good nose for what is to come. One cannot impose styles on these people by a brutal majority decision taken around the green table. The big manufacturer is aware of this, but I believe that the small master hatter too should participate in the favorable turn of the market that has come about for his products. It is on his account then that the Hatters Association, if it feels equal to this difficult task, should take things in hand. But it is possible that even the large manufacturer will refuse. Then the English will be the happy inheritors of the great treasure that the little hatmakers in the Alps have carefully preserved for a thousand years.

For the English have a very different business sense from the Austrians. They produce different hats for each market. We must not succumb to the deception; even the English hat that we get in downtown Vienna is a compromise between the modern hat and the hat of the Hatters Association. Those objects for which

47

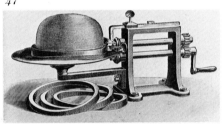

48

47 Three-spindle turning machine by Grahl & Hohl, Dresden. From Carl Bortfeldt, Die Hutmacherkunst: Ein Handbuch für den Klein- und Grossbetrieb, *Leipzig, 1902.*

48 Brim-cutting machine. From Carl Bortfeldt, Die Hutmacherkunst: Ein Handbuch für den Klein- und Grossbetrieb, *1902.*

there is the greatest preference among the barbarians are manufactured for the barbarians. The English treat us like barbarians. And they are right to do so. In this way they sell a great number of hats to us, whereas they would do very bad business here with the hat worn by the most fashionable set. They do not sell to the Viennese the hat which is modern, but rather the hat which the Viennese think is modern. And there is quite a big difference.

The correct hat is only sold in London. When the hat I bought in London wore out, I tried to find one here with the "correct shape." It was then that I discovered that the English hats sold here do not correspond to those sold in London. I had a hatter order me a hat from England of the style that was being worn by members of the royal family. I stipulated that the guarantee of the London firm be included. Cost was immaterial. Well, I had a nice reception! After months of excuses and after a considerable sum of money had already been wired, the English firm called off the transaction completely. For the Hatters Association, however, it would have been an easy thing to acquire these styles. Speed would not have been a problem. We should be very satisfied that we can today buy the hat that English society wore three years ago. For us that hat would still be so ultramodern that no one in Vienna would notice it. And that is what one must ask for in a modern hat. Fashion advances slowly, more slowly than one usually assumes. Objects that are really modern stay so for a long time. But if one hears of an article of clothing that has already become old-fashioned by the following season—that has become, in other words, unpleasantly obvious—then one can assume that it was never modern, but was trying falsely to pass itself off as modern.

If one looks at the products of our hatmaking industry that are on exhibit in the Rotunda, it makes one's heart ache to think that such an excellent industry does not do a greater export business. There is no tastelessness—except for the portrait of the kaiser in the linings of the hats—and even the smallest masters are capable of producing hats that are of the same excellent quality as those of the top houses. This industry is one of the most eminent; unfortunately this cannot be said of any of the other branches of the clothing trade. Every hatter wants to operate according to his own personal standard of excellence and despises the well-known exhibition foolishness of commandeering the attention of the visitors with strange styles. Thereby this entire section of the exhibition has a refined, elegant air. The Hatters Association has assembled twelve exhibitors in one showcase—large and small masters, all excellent in quality. Our firms— Habig, Berger, Ita, and Skrivan—have distinguished themselves by the abundance of their displays. Unfortunately, as to the correctness of their form, I cannot allow myself to give an opinion—I have already been in Vienna for two years. But for elegance of detail work, I would have to give the prize to the hats by Ita.

It would, however, be desirable for our Hatters Association to try to develop contact with the other peoples of culture. The creation of a national Austrian style is an illusion; to cling obstinately to it would cause our industry incalculable damage. China is beginning to tear down its wall, and it is well advised to do so. We must not tolerate the effort of people to erect a great Chinese wall around us out of a false and parochial sense of patriotism.

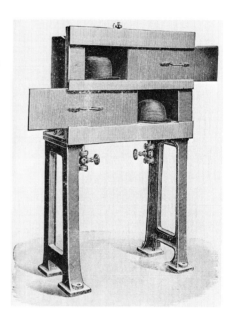

49 Warming cabinet used prior to final shaping. From Carl Bortfeldt, Die Hutmacherkunst: Ein Handbuch für den Klein- und Grossbetrieb, *1902.*

Tempora mutantur, nos et mutamur in illis! Times change and we change with them. Our feet do the same. Sometimes they are small, sometimes large, sometimes pointed, sometimes wide. And so the shoemaker sometimes makes small, sometimes large, sometimes pointed, sometimes wide shoes.

Of course, the form of our feet does not change from season to season. That often requires several centuries, at the very least a generation. A large foot cannot get smaller with a snap of the finger. Here the other clothing artists have it easier. Wide waistlines, narrow waistlines, broad shoulders, narrow shoulders, and so much else—changes can be easily made by means of a new cut, cotton padding, and other aids. But the shoemaker must adhere closely to the form which the foot has at the particular moment. If he wants to introduce the small shoe, he must wait patiently until the race of men with large feet has become extinct.

But of course the feet of all men do not have the same form at the same time. People who use their feet more will have larger feet; those who use them seldom will have smaller ones. What is the shoemaker to do about this? Which type of foot should be his standard? For he will be intent on producing modern shoes. He too wants to be progressive; and he too aspires to acquire the largest possible market for his products.

He sets about it in the same way as all the other trades do. He keeps to the foot-type of those who have power in society. In the Middle Ages, it was the knights who were in power; they were horsemen, men whose feet were smaller than those of the soldiers who went on foot because they frequently sat on their horses. For this reason small feet were modern, and the impression of narrowness, which came to be preferred, was heightened by means of elongation (pointed shoes). But when the knightly class experienced a decline and the pedestrian burghers in the town rose to highest regard, then the large, wide foot of the patrician striding slowly around town came into vogue. In the seventeenth and eighteenth centuries, a distinctly court-oriented life brought the habit of walking again into disrepute; and, because of the widespread use of the sedan chair, the small foot (and thus the small shoe) with high platforms (heels) came back into prevalence. The latter stood one in good stead for the park and the palace, but not for the street.

Recently the revival of Germanic culture has again made riding respectable. All those who thought and felt modern in the last century wore English riding shoes and boots, even if they did not own a horse. The riding boot was the symbol of the free man, who had won a final victory over the buckled shoe, the air of the court, and the glistening parquet floor. Feet still remained small, but the high heel, useless for the horseback rider, was left behind. The whole of the following century, our century, that is, was taken up with the pursuit of the smallest possible foot.

But even in the course of this century the human foot began to undergo a change. Our social circumstances made it necessary for us to walk more quickly each year. Saving time means saving money. Even the most elegant circles, people who had plenty of time, were caught up in it and accelerated their pace. The normal gait of a vigorous pedestrian of today matches that of the footmen running in front of the carriages of the last century. It would be impossible for us to walk as slowly as people did in earlier times. We are too nervous for that. In the eighteenth century soldiers still marched at a pace that looks to us like a kind of continous shifting from foot to foot which would be quite fatiguing. The increase

Footwear

Neue Freie Presse, August 7, 1898

50 Fashion plate from Europäische Moden-Zeitung für Herren-Garderobe, *no. 9, Dresden, 1865. The figures have stylishly small feet.*
51 English riding clothes. From The Tailor and Cutter, *London, 1902. (overleaf)*
52 Scotsman in kilt. From Max von Boehn, Bekleidungskunst und Mode, *Munich, 1918. (overleaf)*
53 English bicycling clothes. From The Illustrated London News, *March 6, 1897. (overleaf)*
54 Poster designed by Alfred Roller for the Vienna Cycling Club. From Ver Sacrum, *no. 1, 1898. (overleaf)*

51

52

in speed is perhaps best illustrated by the fact that the army of Friedrich the Great marched 70 paces per minute, whereas a modern army can march 120 paces per minute. (The drill regulations prescribe a pace of 115 to 117 steps per minute. At present, however, this rate can only be adhered to with effort since the soldiers themselves are pressing for a quicker pace. The new edition of the code will have to take account of precisely this kind of sign of the times.) On this basis it is possible to calculate how many steps per minute our soldiers of a hundred years from now will march, and thereby the speed of all men who want to move ahead quickly.

Nations with a more highly developed culture walk more quickly than those that are still backward; the Americans walk faster than the Italians. When one goes to New York, one always has the feeling that there has been an accident somewhere. In the Kärntnerstrasse today a Viennese citizen of the preceding century would have the similar impression that something must have happened.

We are walking faster. In other words, we are pushing off from the ground with our big toes ever more powerfully. And in fact, our big toes are constantly becoming more powerful and strong. Slow ambling along results in a widening of the foot, whereas brisk walking leads to a lengthening of the foot because of the greater development of the big toe. And since the rest of the toes, especially the little toe, do not keep pace with this development (they actually become stunted from being little used), the foot even begins to become narrower.

The pedestrian has displaced the horseback rider. This only means, of course, a strengthening of the Germanic cultural principle. "Advance under your own power" is the slogan for the next century. The horse was the transition between the sedan chair and one's own self. But our century tells the tale of the horseback rider's rise and fall. It was the true century of the horse. The smell of the stable was our most refined perfume, horse racing our most popular national sport. The rider was the darling of the folk song. The rider's death, the rider's lady-love, the rider's departure. The pedestrian was a nobody. The whole world went about dressed like a rider. And if we wanted to dress very elegantly, we put on our riding coats, our tails. Every student had his nag; the streets were bustling with riders.

How different it is now! The rider is the man of the plains, of the flat lands. He used to be the English free landed gentleman who raised horses and appeared at a meet from time to time to jump over fences after the fox. And now he is replaced by the man who dwells in the mountains, who takes pleasure in scaling the heights, risking his life to elevate himself by his own strength above the homesteads of men: he is the highlander, the Scotsman.

The horseback rider wears boots and long pants (riding breeches) that reach over the knee and should have a very narrow opening there. These are of no use to the person on foot or to the mountain dweller. Whether he lives in Scotland or in the Alps, he wears laced-up shoes and socks that must not reach over the knee; his knees are bare. The Scotsman wears his famous kilt, the Alpine dweller his lederhosen—the principle of both is the same. The materials that the rider and the hiker wear also are different. The man of the plains wears smooth cloth, the man of the mountains rough, woven cloth (homespuns and loden).

Climbing mountains became a necessity for man. The same men who had had such an intense horror of high mountains just a hundred years earlier fled the plains for the mountains. To climb mountains, to convey one's own body upward through one's own strength, is now considered the most noble passion.

But should all those be excluded from this noble passion who do not live in the highlands? Remember that in the previous century it was riding that was considered the noble passion. People sought a means whereby they too could experience something similar; people sought a device whereby the same motion could be carried out on level ground. The bicycle was invented.

The bicyclist is the mountain climber of the plains. That is why he dresses like the climber. He does not need high boots and long pants. He wears pants that are wide around the knee, ending beneath it in cuffs on top of which folded-over stockings are worn. (They are folded over in both Scotland and the Alps so that they will not slip down the leg.) In this way the knee has enough free play underneath the pants so that it is possible to go from a stretched-out leg position to a bent-knee position unimpeded. Incidentally, let me mention here that there are individuals in Vienna who do not at all understand the purpose of the cuffs and who pull their stockings up underneath their cuffs. They make the same comical impression as do the many false natives who render the mountains unsafe every summer in the Alps.

For footwear, the bicyclist wears laced-up shoes like the mountaineer. Shoes with laces will dominate the next century just as riding boots dominated this century. The English have discovered the direct transition; they still wear both kinds today. But we have put out a hideous hybrid for the transitional period: the ankle boot. The most unpleasant thing about the appearance of the ankle boot became obvious when short pants came in. It was clear immediately: one could not wear ankle boots without the beneficent camouflage of long pants. Our officers wore stockings to cover them and were quite unhappy when the uniform regulations were more strictly controlled and stockings were prohibited for the infantry. But basically ankle boots are out, as out as the tail coat when worn in broad daylight, the comical impression of which we notice for the first time when out on the street. In the most oppressive heat we must don our overcoat and ride in a carriage. It's a comical effect—which is precisely what has always caused the downfall of any piece of wearing apparel.

53

In fashionable circles feet are no longer as small as they used to be because of pedestrian activity. They are constantly increasing in size. The big feet of English men and women no longer summon up our mockery. We too climb mountains, have bicycles, and—*horribile dictu*—now have acquired English feet. But let's take comfort. The beauty of the small foot is slowly beginning to fade, especially for men. Recently I received a letter from America with a description of Rigo;[1] it ended by saying, "A pair of revoltingly small feet peeked out from underneath the pants." *Revoltingly* small feet! That sounds convincing. The new teaching begins in America: revoltingly small feet! Holy Clauren,[2] if you had only lived to experience it! You, whose heroes could never have small enough feet to appear as the paragons of noble manhood in the visions and dreams of a hundred thousand German girls! *Tempora mutantur . . .*

54

55

56

When a reply to the article on the activities of the Hatters Association was published in these pages, it was hard to imagine the ramifications of this action. The consequences have now become clear. The interested parties have been overcome by a frenzy of denials. Anyone who is of a different opinion finds it a matter of course that his views too be expressed. Denials of every sort are made. Thus, "Herr S."—who for twenty years has been active in the shoemaking business(!), as he asserts with exclamation points after his signature—"allows himself to request a favorable reception of the following lines of corrective commentary." Thereupon follows a list of paragraphs each beginning with "It is incorrect that . . ."

Perhaps my readers are curious as to just what Herr S. is correcting. Let us pick out a few points at random. It is incorrect, Herr S. asserts, to compare mountain climbing to bicycle riding. Or: it is incorrect that every student has his own nag. Or: it is incorrect that tie shoes will prevail in the next century. A second gentleman, Herr Sch., likewise requests consideration of his few lines in the hope of being able to contribute at least a few things to the resuscitation of our otherwise depressed Austrian shoe industry. In doing so, however, he has suffered a misfortune. He has taken my enthusiastic words dedicated to the Hatters Association at face value, for he polemicizes against my assertion that mountain climbing, marching, and bicycle riding have brought the tie shoe into favor, and then opines, and I quote, "Let us thus look for other reasons. I am thinking here of the lightweight footwear that made the tie shoe so popular. The shoemakers forced the issue with the tie shoe and brought out pretty forms of it. And that's the rub. The shoemaker creates the fashion. Herr Loos recently told us the story of the Hatters Association so nicely, how it determines fashion. It is the same thing here."

Now clearly one can't always expect a favorable reception to everything. The involuntary comic is always amusing. But this paper is not a comic strip. That missive defending the activity of the Hatters Association offered an interesting complement to my attacks and helped to clarify the situation a great deal. It put an end forever to that voting method of theirs in a much stronger and more devastating way than my arguments and reproaches could have. It was stronger and more devastating because it originated in their own camp. The public may well ask what passes for good taste in this camp that determines the style in hats. I have never denied that there are people who consider the styles of the Hatters Association to be quite elegant. But what do these people look like? What kind of taste do they have? Herr Kessler's letter expresses it very precisely. He considers it compatible with his taste that the portrait of His Majesty is printed inside the lining of a hat. In doing so, he evokes Bukovina,[1] where portraits of national heroes are treated in a similar fashion. So now it should be clear to the public. On the one hand England, on the other Bukovina!

The letters from the gentlemen in the shoe business, however, do not contribute in any way to clarifying the issue. In general they all amount to the same thing, that the endorsement of the tie shoe will damage the Austrian shoemaking industry since the tie shoe will displace the ankle boot which, strange to say, is considered the Austrian national shoe. Such an accusation is certainly untenable. For shoes and boots are both worn regardless of whether they are of one style or the other. It is a matter of indifference to the shoemaker. Not so for the elastic manufacturers, who just now must begin to think about producing other products. No man can work against the march of the times; fifty million kilograms of printer's ink can no longer revive the ankle boot.

Shoemakers

Neue Freie Presse, August 14, 1898

55 Page from The London Shoe Company Catalogue, *London, c. 1890, advertising women's cycling boots and shoes.*
56 Page from The London Shoe Company Catalogue, *London, c. 1890, advertising men's riding boots and tie shoes.*

The exhibition itself really teaches this to us. In the display window of the Shoemakers Union, we can count only three pairs of ladies' ankle boots, three pairs of men's ankle boots, and three pairs of uniform ankle boots among the 192 pairs of shoes brought to the exhibition. These statistics bespeak a cruel truth. And in ten years? We shall look for even these last nine pairs of boots in vain.

According to the English shoemakers, our shoemakers may well make the best shoes in the world. Many outstanding shoemakers can be enumerated in the various capitals of Europe, but the typical skilled worker on the average ranks the Austrians—as far as footwear goes—over every other national people. This is all the more amazing since our shoemakers are very badly paid for their work. The public increasingly drives down the prices, and the deficit must be made up for in the shoes themselves if the craftsman is not to be ruined. But do not think that it makes the shoemaker happy to produce shoes of poor quality. You force him to it. He dreams of using the best leather and working it in the best manner. How gladly he would spend one day more on a pair of shoes! And how it pains him to force his assistants to work more quickly, knowing full well that because of the speed, many a careless piece of work will have to go unreprimanded. But life is relentless. He must, must, must produce shoes at a certain price, and so he must make the difficult decision to fire the good but slow worker and to economize with his raw materials. It already begins with the thread. But you, those of you who take a special pleasure in tricking your shoemaker out of another gulden and then readily spend it for a better armchair at the theater when your customary seats are sold out, you are the worst enemies of our crafts industry! Haggling, bargaining, pushing prices down—all have a demoralizing effect on both producer and consumer.

But even so there are good shoes. Our shoemakers are simply capable men. There remain much spirit and personality in them. It is not by chance that the greatest poet and the greatest philosopher to have been bestowed on us by the artisan class were shoemakers. How many Hans Sachses and Jakob Böhmes have sat and still sit on the shoemaker's stool,[2] who have thought and felt the same way, but have never written a word? Maybe that is why the Germans have such good shoemakers, since every able and individualistic (and thus in his parents' opinion naughty) young boy is warned, "If you don't obey, you'll be apprenticed to a shoemaker!" And it often comes true.

Less praiseworthy are our shoe *wearers*. I mentioned in my last essay that the shoemaker must make his shoes conform to the type of feet possessed by the dominant social class. It is to these feet that the shoes are fit. But people whose feet do not have this shape still demand the same style from their shoemakers. The result is numerous crippled feet, something one can only find among those people who do *not* belong to the dominant social class. For their vanity, however, the shoemaker is held responsible. The low prices do not allow him to fashion each shoe individually for the customer. Thus even if an old last might be made to fit by forcing it, the shoemaker cannot obtain an accurate line for the shoe, upon which an even tread depends. This accurate line of the sole of the shoe—probably one of the most difficult tasks of shoemaking—is not determined by the outline of the foot, but for the most part by the gait and walking habits of the wearer.

Shoemakers who produce expensive shoes unfortunately make a smaller profit than those who set out from the start to produce inferior goods. Let us take, for example, the eighteen-gulden shoemaker and the six-gulden shoemaker. The

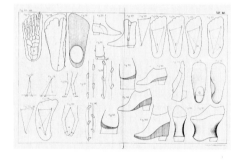

57 Diagram illustrating how foot shape and walking habits affect normal and corrective shoemaking. From Bernhard Rodegast, Die Fusskleidungskunst, *Vienna, 1905.*

first has a last cut that costs six gulden including his own work. He has the upper part made by an assistant, to whom he pays three gulden a day in consideration for his excellent work, and on the material for this upper part he spends three gulden. The six-gulden shoemaker takes an old last and orders the upper part from the factory for about two gulden. In this way, the first spends sixty-six percent, the second thirty-three percent of the whole price of the shoe. But too little also is done for the preservation of the shoes. By trying to save the money that a good shoe tree costs, one wears out more shoes than do those who put shoe trees in their shoes overnight.

The exhibition displays only honest shoewear since "indecent" shoes have been banned. That it took the decency code to eliminate shoes that served no other purpose than to attract the attention of spectators is regrettable. It would have been much more respectable for the whole industry if these shoes had been rejected from the very beginning because of their uselessness. We want to see what our shoemakers can do, their honest and sound work, not their self-advertisement. An exhibition should be a celebration of work and not of advertising. But wait. The "indecent" shoes are still fated to be represented by three pairs. These are made like walking shoes. They have green *peluche* soles, and one pair of them is even provided with gold lettering after the fashion of old bookbindings.

Our minds may be set at rest. We Austrians will be able to step out smartly in our shoes in the upcoming century. And good shoes will be necessary in the next century because we are going to be on the march. The American Walt Whitman, the greatest Germanic poet since Goethe, has seen this century with a prophetic eye. He sings:

58 Fashionable women's shoes. From
Der Bazar: Illustrierte Damen
Zeitung, *Berlin, December 14, 1891.*

Have the elder races halted?
Do they droop and end their lesson, wearied over there beyond the seas?
We take up the task eternal, and the burden and the lesson,
Pioneers! O pioneers!

All the past we leave behind,
We debouch upon a newer mightier world, varied world,
Fresh and strong the world we seize, world of labor and the march,
Pioneers! O pioneers![3]

No, we are not standing still, old Walt Whitman. The ancient Germanic blood still flows in our veins, and we are ready to march forward. We will do our best to help change the world of sitters and standers into a world of work and of marching.

61

*59 Crayon sketch of an interor with
fireplace. Adolf Loos, c. 1899.*

Which is worth more, a kilogram of stone or a kilogram of gold? The question probably seems ridiculous. But only to the merchant. The artist will answer: All materials are equally valuable as far as I am concerned.

Building Materials

Neue Freie Presse, *August 28, 1898*

The Venus of Milo would be equally valuable whether it were made of the rubble which paved the streets—in Paros, the streets were paved with Parian marble—or gold. The Sistine Madonna would not be worth a penny more if Raphael had mixed a few pounds of gold into his colors. A merchant who has to consider melting down the golden Venus in case of need or scraping off the Sistine Madonna will, of course, calculate differently.

The artist has only one ambition: to master his material in such a way that his work is independent of the value of the raw material. Our architects, however, have not heard of this ambition. For them, a square meter of wall surface out of granite is more valuable than a square meter out of plaster.

But granite in and of itself is worthless. It lies all around outside in the fields; anyone can get hold of it. It forms whole mountains, whole mountain ranges, which one has only to dig up. The streets are topped with it, and the cities are paved with it. It is the most common stone, the most ordinary material that we know. And yet there are people who consider granite our most precious building material.

These people say "material" but they mean "work." Human labor, technical skill, and artistry. For granite demands much work to wrest it from the mountains, much work to bring it to the designated location, work to give it the correct form and to endow it with a pleasing appearance by cutting and polishing. Our hearts beat with reverential awe at the sight of the polished granite wall. Awe for the material? No, awe for the human work.

So might granite then be more valuable than plaster? We have still not said that. For a wall with a plaster decoration by the hand of Michelangelo would overshadow even the most highly polished granite wall. It is not just the quantity, but the quality of the work performed that determines the value of an object.

We live in a time that gives precedence to the quantity of work performed. For quantity is easily controlled; it is immediately obvious to anyone and demands no skilled eye or special knowledge. Thus there are no errors. So many workers have worked at a job for so many hours at such and such a wage. Anyone can calculate it. And we want to make the value of the things with which we surround ourselves easy to understand. Or else there would be no point to them. Thus, those things that took a longer time to make must deserve more respect.

It was not always this way. Formerly one built with the materials that were the most easily obtainable. In some regions this was with brick, in some with stone; in some the walls were stuccoed. Did those who used stucco consider themselves somewhat inferior to those architects who built in stone? Of course not, why should they have? The idea did not occur to anyone. If there were quarries in the vicinity, one simply built out of stone. But to bring stone to a building from far away seemed more a matter of money than of art. And art, the quality of a work, meant more formerly than it does today.

Times like those brought out proud, strong natures in the field of architecture. Fischer von Erlach did not need granite to make himself understood. He created works out of clay, limestone, and sand, works that capture our attention as powerfully as the best buildings made out of materials that are the most difficult to handle. His spirit, his artistry mastered the most miserable materials. He was capable of bestowing the nobility of art on the most plebeian dust. He was a *king* in the realm of materials.

Today it is not the artist who rules, but rather the day laborer, not the creative idea, but the working hours. And the rulership is gradually being wrested even from the hands of the day laborer, for something has appeared that has a quantitatively better and cheaper work output: the machine.

But any amount of production time, whether of the machine or the coolie, costs money. And if one has no money? Then one begins to fake the working hours and to imitate materials.

The reverence for the quantity of work done is the most fearsome enemy that the crafts profession has. For it results in imitation. And imitation has demoralized a large part of our crafts. All pride, all handicraft spirit have left it. "Book printer, what can you do?" "I can print books in such a way that they are taken for lithographs." "And lithographer, what can you do?" "I can make lithographs that are taken for prints." "Carpenter, what can you do?" "I can carve ornaments that look so easy you could mistake them for stuccowork." "And stuccoworker, what can you do?" "I can imitate moldings and ornaments exactly and make hairline joints that appear so authentic that they look like the best stonemasonry." "But I can do that too!" cries the sheet-metal worker proudly. "When my ornaments are painted and sanded, no one would suspect that they are made out of tin." What a pitiful group!

A spirit of self-degradation pervades our crafts. It is no surprise that this profession is doing badly. Such people cannot help but do badly. Carpenter, be proud that you are a carpenter! It is the stuccoworker who makes ornaments. You should pass him by without jealousy or envy. And you, stuccoworker, what have you to do with the stonemason? The stonemason makes joints, unfortunately has to make joints, since little stones are cheaper to come by than big ones. Be proud of the fact that your work does not exhibit the paltry joints that cut the stonemason's columns, ornaments, and walls into sections. Be proud of your profession, be happy that you are not a stonemason!

But I am talking to the wind. The public does not want a proud craftsman. For the better the craftsman can imitate, the more the public will support him. Reverence for expensive materials—the surest sign of the parvenu stage in which our nation currently finds itself—will have it no other way. The parvenu considers it disgraceful not to be able to adorn himself with diamonds, disgraceful not to be able to wear furs, disgraceful not to be able to live in a stone palace—ever since he has learned that diamonds, furs, and stone palaces cost a great deal of money. He does not know that the lack of diamonds, furs, and stone facades has no effect on elegance. Therefore, since he is short of money, he grasps for surrogates. A ridiculous enterprise. For those people whom he wants to deceive, those, that is, endowed with the means to surround themselves with diamonds, furs, and stone facades, cannot be fooled. They find his efforts laughable. And his efforts are further unnecessary vis-à-vis those of a lower standing than his if he is conscious of his own superiority anyway.

In the last decade imitation has dominated the entire building industry. Wall

64

coverings are made out of paper, but this they may by no means show. They must retain the patterns of damask silk or Gobelin tapestries. Doors and windows are made out of softwood. But since hardwood is more expensive, the softwood must be painted to look like it. Iron must be painted to look like bronze or copper. But against poured cement, an achievement of this century, we are entirely helpless. Since cement is in and of itself a splendid material, we have just one thought whenever we use it, the same thought that we have upon first confronting any new material: what can we imitate with it? We used it as a surrogate for stone. And since poured cement is so extremely inexpensive, like the parvenus that we are, we indulged in the most thoroughgoing wastefulness. A true cement epidemic gripped the century. "Oh, my dear Herr Architect, couldn't you put just a little more art on the facade for another five gulden?" the vain contractor probably said. And the architect tacked as many gulden worth of art onto the facade as were demanded of him, and sometimes a little more.

Nowadays poured cement is being utilized for the imitation of stuccowork. It is characteristic of our Viennese situation that I who am against the violation of materials, who have combated imitation energetically, am dismissed as being a "materialist." Just look at the sophistry: these are the people who attribute such a value to materials that they have no fear of their becoming characterless and who freely resort to surrogates.

The English have exported their wallpaper to us. Unfortunately they cannot send over entire houses as well. But we can see from their wallpaper just what the English are aiming for. This is wallpaper that is not ashamed to be made of paper. And why should it be? There are certain wall coverings that cost more. But the Englishman is not a parvenu. In his home, it could never occur to anyone that the money had run out. Likewise, his clothes are made of sheep's wool, and they display this honestly. If the leadership in clothing were left to the Viennese, sheep's wool would be woven to look like velvet and satin. Even though it is only made out of wool, English clothing material, and thus our clothing material, never manifests the Viennese "I'd really like it, but I can't afford it."

And that should bring us to a chapter that plays the most important role in architecture, to a principle that should form the ABC of every architect—namely the principle of cladding. But I will reserve discussion of this principle for my next article.

The Principle of Cladding

Neue Freie Presse, *September 4, 1898*

Even if all materials are of equal value to the artist, they are not equally suited to all his purposes. The requisite durability, the necessary construction often demand materials that are not in harmony with the true purpose of the building. The architect's general task is to provide a warm and livable space. Carpets are warm and livable. He decides for this reason to spread out one carpet on the floor and to hang up four to form the four walls. But you cannot build a house out of carpets. Both the carpet on the floor and the tapestry on the wall require a structural frame to hold them in the correct place. To invent this frame is the architect's second task.

This is the correct and logical path to be followed in architecture. It was in this sequence that mankind learned how to build. In the beginning was cladding.[1] Man sought shelter from inclement weather and protection and warmth while he slept. He sought to cover himself. The covering is the oldest architectural detail. Originally it was made out of animal skins or textile products. This meaning of the word is still known today in the Germanic languages.[2] Then the covering had to be put up somewhere if it was to afford enough shelter to a family! Thus the walls were added, which at the same time provided protection on the sides. In this way the idea of architecture developed in the minds of mankind and individual men.

There are architects who do things differently. Their imaginations create not spaces but sections of walls. That which is left over around the walls then forms the rooms. And for these rooms some kind of cladding is subsequently chosen, whatever seems fitting to the architect.

But the artist, the *architect*, first senses the effect that he intends to realize and sees the rooms he wants to create in his mind's eye. He senses the effect that he wishes to exert upon the spectator: fear and horror if it is a dungeon, reverence if a church, respect for the power of the state if a government palace, piety if a tomb, homeyness if a residence, gaiety if a tavern. These effects are produced by both the material and the form of the space.

Every material possesses its own language of forms, and none may lay claim for itself to the forms of another material. For forms have been constituted out of the applicability and the methods of production of materials. They have come into being with and through materials. No material permits an encroachment into its own circle of forms. Whoever dares to make such an encroachment notwithstanding this is branded by the world a counterfeiter. Art, however, has nothing to do with counterfeiting or lying. Her paths are full of thorns, but they are pure.

One could cast St. Stefan's Tower in cement and erect it somewhere, but then it would not be a work of art. And what goes for the Stefan's Tower also goes for the Pitti Palace; and what goes for the Pitti Palace goes for the Farnese Palace. And with this building we have arrived in the midst of our own Ringstrasse architecture. It was a sad time for art, a sad time for those few artists among the architects of that time who were forced to prostitute their art for the sake of the masses. It was granted to only a small number consistently to find contractors broad-minded enough to let the artist have his way. Schmidt was probably the luckiest. After him came Hansen, who, when he was having a rough time, sought solace in terra-cotta buildings. Poor Ferstel must have endured terrible agonies when they forced him at the last minute to nail an entire section of facade in poured cement onto his University.[3] The remaining architects of this period—

with a few exceptions—knew how to keep themselves free of nightmarish agonies like these.

Is it any different now? Allow me to answer this question. Imitation and surrogate art still dominate architecture. Yes, more than ever. In recent years people have even appeared who have lent themselves to defending this tendency (one person, of course, did so anonymously, since the issue did not seem clear-cut enough to him); so that the surrogate architect no longer need stand diminutively on the sidelines. Nowadays one nails the structure to the facade with aplomb and hangs the "keystone" under the main molding with artistic authority. But come hither, you heralds of imitation, you makers of stenciled inlays, of botch-up-your-home windows and papier-mâché tankards! There is a new spring awakening for you in Vienna! The earth is freshly fertilized!

But is the living space that has been constructed entirely of rugs not an imitation? The walls are not really built out of carpets! Certainly not. But these carpets are meant only to be carpets and not building stones. They were never meant to be taken as such, to imitate them in form or color, but rather to reveal clearly their own meaning as a cladding for the wall surface. They fulfill their purpose according to the principles of cladding.

As I already mentioned at the outset, cladding is older even than structure. The reasons for cladding things are numerous. At times it is a protection against bad weather—oil-base paint, for example, on wood, iron, or stone; at times there are hygienic reasons for it—as in the case of enameled tiles that cover the wall surfaces in the bathroom; at times it is the means to a specific effect—as in the color painting of statues, the tapestries on walls, the veneer on wood. The principle of cladding, which was first articulated by Semper, extends to nature as well. Man is covered with skin, the tree with bark.

60 Vienna tramcar at the turn of the century. From Paul Kortz, Wien am Anfang des XX Jahrhunderts. Ein Führer in Technischer und Künstlerischer Richtung, hrsg. vom Österreichisches Ingenieur- und Architekten-Verein, Vienna, 1905-1906.

From the principle of cladding, however, I have derived a very precise law which I call the law of cladding. Do not be alarmed. It is usually said that laws put an end to all progressive development. And indeed, the old masters got along perfectly well without laws. Certainly. It would be idleness to establish laws against thievery in a place where thievery is unknown. When the materials used for cladding had not yet been imitated, there was no need for laws. But now it seems to me to be high time for them.

The law goes like this: we must work in such a way that a confusion of the material clad with its cladding is impossible. That means, for example, that wood may be painted any color except one—the color of wood. In a city where the exhibition committee decided that all of the wood in the Rotunda should be painted "like mahogany," in a city in which wood graining is the exclusive type of painted decoration, this is a very daring law. There seem to be people here who consider this kind of thing elegant. Since the railway and tramway cars—as well as the entire technique of carriage building—come from England, they are the only wooden objects that display pure colors. I now dare to assert that this kind of tramcar—especially one of the electric line—is more pleasing to me with its pure colors than it would be if, according to the principles of beauty set out by the exhibition committee, it had been painted "like mahogany."

But a true feeling for elegance lies dormant, although deep and buried, even in our people. If not, the railway administration could not count on the fact that the brown color of the third-class cars painted to look like wood would call forth a

67

lesser feeling of elegance than the green color of the second- and first-class cars.

I once demonstrated this unconscious feeling to one of my colleagues in a drastic manner. On the first floor of a building there were two apartments. The tenant of the one apartment had had his window bars, which had been stained brown, painted white at his own expense. We made a bet according to which we brought a certain number of people to the front of the building and, without pointing out to them the difference between the window bars, asked them on which side they felt that Herr Pluntzengruber lived and on which side Prince Liechtenstein— these were the two parties that we told them rented the apartments. All of those who were taken to the building unanimously declared that the wood-stained side was Pluntzengruber's. Since then my colleague has only painted things white.

Wood staining is, of course, an invention of our century. The Middle Ages painted wood bright red for the most part, the Renaissance blue; the Baroque and Rococo painted interiors white, exteriors green. Our peasants still retain enough good sense to paint only with pure colors. Don't the green gate and the green fence of the countryside, the green jalousies against the freshly whitewashed wall, have a charming effect? Unfortunately several villages have already adopted the taste of the exhibition commission.

One will still recall the moral indignation that arose in the camp of the surrogate arts and crafts when the first furniture painted with oil-base paint came to Vienna from England. But the rage of these good men was not directed against the paint. They painted with oil-base paints in Vienna too as soon as softwood came into use. But the fact that the English pieces dared to display their colors so openly and freely instead of imitating hardwood provoked these strange fellows. They rolled their eyes and acted as if they had never used oil-base colors at all. These gentlemen presumably thought that everyone hitherto had assumed their stained-wood furniture and buildings were actually made of hardwood.

I trust I can be assured of the Association's gratitude if, after such observations, I name no names among the painters at the exhibition.

Applied to stuccowork, the principle of cladding would run like this: stucco can take any ornament with just one exception—rough brickwork. One would think the declaration of such a self-evident fact to be unnecessary, but just recently someone drew my attention to a building whose plaster walls were painted red and then seamed with white lines. Similarly, the type of decoration so beloved in kitchens—imitation stone squares—belongs in this category. In general, any and all materials used to cover walls—wallpaper, oilcloth, fabric, or tapestries— ought not to aspire to represent squares of brick or stone. It is thus easy to understand why the legs of our dancers when covered with knit stockinets have such an unaesthetic effect. Woven underclothing may be dyed any color at all, just not skin color.

The cladding material can keep its natural color if the area to be covered happens to be of the same color. Thus, I can smear tar on black iron or cover wood with another wood (veneer, marquetry, and so on) without having to color the covering wood; I can coat one metal with another by heating or galvanizing it. But the principle of cladding forbids the cladding material to imitate the coloration of the underlying material. Thus iron can be tarred, painted with oil colors, or galvanized, but it can never be camouflaged with a bronze color or any other metallic color.

Here *chamottes*[4] and artificial stone tiles also deserve mention. The one kind imitates terrazzo (mosaic) paving, the other Persian carpets. Certainly there are people who actually take the tiles for what they are imitating—for the manufacturers must know their customers.

But no, you imitators and surrogate architects, you are mistaken! The human soul is too lofty and sublime for you to be able to dupe it with your tactics and tricks. Of course, our pitiful bodies are in your power. They have only five senses at their disposal to distinguish real from counterfeit. And at that point where the man with his sense organs is no longer adequate begins your true domain. There is your realm. But even here—you are mistaken once more! Paint the best inlays high, high up on the wood ceiling and our poor eyes will have to take it on good faith perhaps. But the divine spirits will not be fooled by your tricks. They sense that even those intarsia decorations most skillfully painted to look "like inlay" are nothing but oil paint.

**Nightdresses, Chemises
Combinations, Skirts**

TAUSKY & MANDL

WIEN, I. WIPPLINGERSTRASSE 16
ECKE SCHWERTGASSE

MEINE HERREN!

Es gereicht mir zum Vergnügen, Ihnen mit-
teilen zu können, daß ich Gelegenheit hatte,
die von Ihrer Firma erzeugten Wäschestücke
zu begutachten. Ich finde, daß dieselben in
praktischer Ausführung und hygienischer Hin-
sicht den Anforderungen höchster Kultur ent-
sprechen. Durch den Bestand Ihrer Firma ist
man nicht mehr genötigt Night-gowns and
Combinations in England zu bestellen. ◎◎◎
WIEN, 12. August 1902.

Hochachtungsvoll ADOLF LOOS

61 Advertisement by the firm of Tausky & Mandl for women's nightdresses, chemises, combinations, and skirts. Adolf Loos's endorsement reads, "Gentlemen! It gives me great pleasure to be able to inform you that I have had the opportunity to evaluate articles of underclothing manufactured by your firm. I find these articles to be of serviceable quality and hygienic with respect to the requirements of the highest standards of culture. Because of your firm's existence, it is no longer necessary to order nightgowns and combinations from England." From Das Andere, no. 1, 1903.

I recently got into a quarrel with an acquaintance of mine. He did not dispute what I had written about the arts and crafts. But the essays on fashion and clothing had rubbed him the wrong way. He reproached me for wanting to put the whole world into uniform. "What would become of our splendid national costumes?"

Here he became poetic. He thought about his childhood, the lovely Sundays in Linz; he thought of the local folk who assembled for church in their festive attire. How glorious, how beautiful, how picturesque! How different everything is now! Only the old people cling to the old costumes. The young ape the ways of city people. One ought instead try to win the people back to the old costume. That would be the task of the cultured and literate man.

"So you think they liked this old costume?" I interjected. "Certainly." "And so you wish that this costume would be retained forever?" "It is my most ardent desire."

Now I had him where I wanted him. "Do you realize," I said to him, "that you are a truly base and egotistical man? Do you realize that you want to exclude an entire class, a large, wonderful class, our peasant class, from all of the blessings of culture? And why? So that your eyes will be picturesquely titillated as soon as you make your way into the countryside! Why do *you* not run about dressed that way? No thank you, you say, I would just as soon not. But you demand that other people oblige you by gadding about in the countryside like figures in a landscape just so that your drunken intellectual's eyes will not be offended. Well then, why don't you take their place there sometime, serving up country sausages to His Excellency the Commerce Minister who wants to enjoy the untainted mountain pastures? The peasant has a higher mission to fulfill than to populate the mountains stylishly for the holiday visitor. The peasant—so the saying has already gone for a hundred years—is not a plaything!"

I too admit that I really take pleasure in the old costumes. But this does not give me the right to demand from my fellow man that he put them on for my sake. A costume is clothing that has frozen in a particular form; it will develop no further. It is always a sign that its wearer has given up trying to change his circumstances. The costume is the symbol of resignation. It says, my wearer must give up seeking to gain a better position for himself in the struggle for existence; he must give up trying to develop himself further. When the peasant still fought with vim and vigor, when he was still full of the greenest hopes, he would never even have dreamed of putting on the same suit that his grandfather had worn. The Middle Ages, the Peasants' War, the Renaissance—these eras knew no rigid adherence to clothing styles. It was only the different ways of life that caused the distinction between the clothing of the city dweller and the peasant. City dweller and peasant at that time related to one another like today's city dweller and farmer.

But then the peasant lost his independence. He became a serf. And a serf he had to remain, he and his children and his children's children. To what purpose should he strive to raise himself above his surroundings by means of his clothing, for what should he modify his style of dress? For it was of no use at all. The peasant class became a caste; the peasant was deprived of every hope of leaving this caste behind. Peoples that have separated into castes all have one trait in common: they all cling rigidly for thousands of years to their native costume.

Underclothes

Neue Freie Presse, *September 25, 1898*

Then the peasant became free. But only externally. Internally he still felt inferior to the city dweller. The latter was the master. The hundreds of years of servitude were still too much in the peasant's bones.

But now a new generation arises. It has declared war on the costume. In doing so it has a good ally—the threshing machine. Wherever the threshing machine wages its campaign, it is over forever for the picturesque old clothes. They now are going just where they belong: to the costume-hiring agency.

These are heartless words. But they must be spoken, for there have even been clubs formed in Austria out of false sentimentality that endeavor to preserve for the peasant the stigma of his servitude. Clubs that supported exactly the opposite would be much more indispensable. For even we city dwellers are still at a very far remove from the clothing that the great civilized nations wear. Of course on the outside we look quite passable. There we could hold our own with the others. We could manage, if we allowed ourselves to be dressed by one of the top Viennese tailors, to be taken for civilized Europeans on the sidewalks of London, New York, or Peking. But woe to us if the top layers of our clothing fell off piece by piece and we stood there in our underclothes! Then everyone would realize that we simply put on our European clothes like a mask, and that underneath we still wear the national costume.

But it is either/or. We have to decide. Either we have the courage of our convictions to differentiate ourselves from the rest of mankind and dress in a national costume, or we want to cling to the rest of humanity and dress as they do. But it certainly lacks refinement to play the cultivated individual only on the outside, to seek to dissimulate by means of the articles of clothing that are within the stranger's view.

While our top layer of clothing separates us by a whole world from the peasant, our undergarments, our underclothes, are exactly the same as those of the peasant. In Budapest they wear the same underpants as the *csikos;*[1] in Vienna people wear the same underpants as the Lower Austrian farmer. What is it then that so much separates us in terms of our underwear from the rest of the civilized nations?

The fact is that we lag at least fifty years behind the stage in which England finds itself at present. There, knit underclothes have vanquished woven underclothes. We have had no great revolutions to take note of in the course of this century in terms of the top layers of clothing. All the more decisive have they been in underclothes. A century ago people still wrapped themselves entirely in linen. But in the course of this century we have gradually set about restoring to the knitwear manufacturer his proper domain. We proceeded step by step, from one part of the body to the next. We began with the feet, and then moved upward. At present, the work of the knitter is directed to the whole lower portion of the body. Meanwhile the upper body must still put up with the fact that a linen undershirt takes the place of a knit one.

We began with the feet. In this area we have also made progress. We no longer wear foot wrappings but stockings. Yet we still wear linen underpants, an article of clothing already extinct in England and America.

If a man came to Vienna from the Balkan states, where they still wear foot wrappings, and went in search of a lingerie shop where he could buy his customary

MEN'S NORMAL SANATORY DRAWERS,
IN NATURAL GRAY WOOL.
DOUBLE THICKNESS OVER THE CHEST AND ABDOMEN.

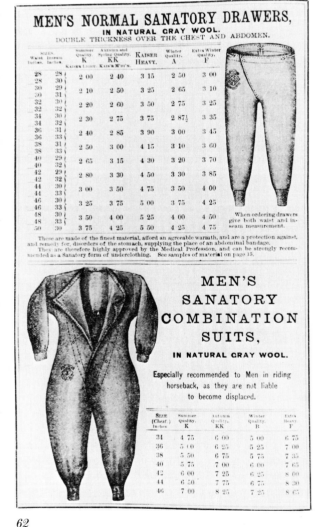

SIZES Waist Inches.	Inseam Inches.	Summer Quality. K KAISER LIGHT.	Autumn Spring Quality. KK KAIS'R M'DI'M.	KAISER HEAVY.	Winter Quality. A	Extra Winter Quality. F
28	28	2 00	2 40	3 15	2 50	3 00
28	30					
30	29	2 10	2 50	3 25	2 65	3 10
30	31					
32	30	2 20	2 60	3 50	2 75	3 25
32	32					
34	30	2 30	2 75	3 75	2 87½	3 35
34	32					
36	31	2 40	2 85	3 90	3 00	3 45
36	33					
38	31	2 50	3 00	4 15	3 10	3 60
38	33					
40	29	2 65	3 15	4 30	3 20	3 70
40	32					
42	29	2 80	3 30	4 50	3 30	3 85
42	32					
44	30	3 00	3 50	4 75	3 50	4 00
44	33					
46	30	3 25	3 75	5 00	3 75	4 25
46	33					
48	30	3 50	4 00	5 25	4 00	4 50
48	33					
50	30	3 75	4 25	5 50	4 25	4 75

When ordering drawers give both waist and inseam measurement.

These are made of the finest material, afford an agreeable warmth, and are a protection against, and remedy for, disorders of the stomach, supplying the place of an abdominal bandage.

They are therefore highly approved by the Medical Profession, and can be strongly recommended as a Sanatory form of underclothing. See samples of material on page 15.

MEN'S SANATORY COMBINATION SUITS,
IN NATURAL GRAY WOOL.

Especially recommended to Men in riding horseback, as they are not liable to become displaced.

Size (Chest) Inches	Summer Quality. K	Autumn Quality. KK	Winter Quality. B	Extra Heavy. F
34	4 75	6 00	5 00	6 75
36	5 00	6 25	5 25	7 00
38	5 50	6 75	5 75	7 35
40	5 75	7 00	6 00	7 65
42	6 00	7 25	6 25	8 00
44	6 50	7 75	6 75	8 30
46	7 00	8 25	7 25	8 65

MEN'S SOCKS,

Of Finest, Long-Staple, Four-Threaded, Woolen Yarn: Natural Undyed, or Sanitarily Dyed if in Colors.

Those, who have hitherto worn the cotton or the mixed-cotton-and-wool socks, will find a most agreeable contrast in the use of the fine All-Wool Sock especially manufactured for the Jaeger System.

In our complete stock of Hosiery, in ordinary form, rights and lefts, with one toe or divisions for five toes, and in the different weights and colors, a variety will be found to suit the most fastidious taste.

	Sizes	9	9½	10	10½	11	11½
2249—Rights and lefts, *natural* color; very heavy ...					75		
504— " " " medium heavy,					75		
580—Ordinary shape, " fine..................					50		
690—Rights and lefts, " ; also *black* "O.F."					65		
550— " " " and ordinary shape, *natural*; fine and heavy.....................					75		
550—Ordinary shape, *black*; fine and heavy..........					75		
364—Rights and lefts, *natural*; plain and heavy.....					75		

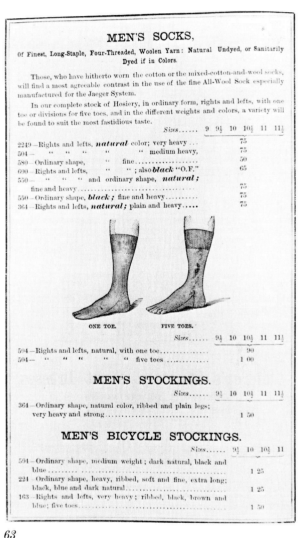

ONE TOE.   **FIVE TOES.**

	Sizes	9½	10	10½	11	11½
504—Rights and lefts, natural, with one toe..............					90	
504— " " " " five toes					1 00	

MEN'S STOCKINGS.

	Sizes	9½	10	10½	11	11½
364—Ordinary shape, natural color, ribbed and plain legs; very heavy and strong............................					1 50	

MEN'S BICYCLE STOCKINGS.

	Sizes	9½	10	10½	11
504—Ordinary shape, medium weight; dark natural, black and blue..				1 25	
224—Ordinary shape, heavy, ribbed, soft and fine, extra long; black, blue and dark natural......................				1 25	
163—Rights and lefts, very heavy; ribbed, black, brown and blue; five toes........................				1 50	

62

63

62 Page from Illustrated Catalogue and Price List of Doctor Jaeger's Sanitary Woolen System Company, *New York, 1887.*
63 Page from Illustrated Catalogue and Price List of Doctor Jaeger's Sanitary Woolen System Company, *featuring models of men's socks with one toe and five toes.*

foot covering, he would be met with the news—incomprehensible to him—that foot wrappings cannot be bought in Vienna. He could, of course, order them. "Well, what do people wear here then?" "Socks." "Socks? Why, they are very uncomfortable. And too hot in the summer. Doesn't anyone wear foot wrappings anymore?" "Oh, yes, the very old people. But the young people find foot wrappings uncomfortable." And so the good man from the Balkans decides with a heavy heart to make the attempt to wear socks. In doing so, he arrives at a new rung of human culture.

Philippopolis[2] is to Vienna as Vienna is to New York. In the latter city, then, let us try to buy—not foot wrappings, for no one would understand us at all—but rather linen underpants. I must ask the reader to reread the preceding conversation once again and for "the man from the Balkan states" substitute "the Viennese man," and for "foot wrappings" substitute "linen underpants." For the conversation would wind up exactly the same way! I am speaking from personal experience. I have heard the original of this conversation, the one concerning the foot wrappings, so spoken that it is comprehensible only in the Viennese context.

Whoever finds woven material more comfortable than knit material, let him continue to wear it forever. For it would be foolish to impose a form of culture on someone, a form of culture that does not correspond to his innermost essence. The fact is that for the man of high culture, linen has become uncomfortable. And so we must bide our time until it begins to become uncomfortable for us Austrians too. It was the increasing participation in physical exercise, in sports activities that came from England, that resulted in the growing aversion to linen underclothes. The starched dickey, collar, and cuffs also are a hindrance to the sportsman. And the unstarched dickey is the forerunner of the unstarched collar. Both of them have the sole task of paving the way for the knit shirt and the flannel shirt.

Knit underclothes, however, do signal one great danger. They are really only meant for people who want to wash for the sake of their own cleanliness. But many Germans see in the wearing of knit underclothes a carte blanche for not having to wash anymore. All inventions designed to cut down on washing originate in Germany. From Germany came cellulose-fiber underclothes, the fake shirtfront, and the tie with an attached dickey made out of the same fabric. In Germany originates the lesson that washing is not beneficial to one's health and that one can wear the same knit shirt for years—so long as one's acquaintances do not positively forbid it. An American cannot imagine a German without his fresh white but fake dickey. This is manifested in the caricature of the German which the American comic strips have correctly presented. The German can be recognized by the tip of his dickey, which always peeks out from his waistcoat. It is only the second-class citizens in American comics who wear fake shirtfronts: the tramp, the vagabond.

The false dickey is truly no symbol of angelical cleanliness. It is all the more unpleasant that this article of clothing, which so pitifully testifies to the cultural position of a people, is to be found in the section of the exhibition in which our best tailors have their displays. It lowers the level of that entire elegant section.

A new commercial type is represented by the "tailors and outfitters." The outfitter stocks everything that pertains to a man's attire. It is no easy task. He is responsible to the buyer for creating a fashionable impression with every article

64 Joseph Olbrich in characteristically stylish suit and tie, circa 1900.

that he sells. One can demand from a well-run fashion shop that one be able to grab from its shelves at random without coming up with anything tasteless or unrefined. The outfitter must make no concessions to the masses. The excuse that other kinds of tastes must be attended to as well should never be used by first-rate businesses. They should never make a mistake. Once the outfitter does happen to make a mistake, he is obligated to his customers no longer to carry the article in question.

It is difficult to win the leading role in the fashion business, but it is still more difficult to keep it. And yet only the minority of goods are manufactured in the outfitter's workshop. He is primarily a retailer. His relationship to the craftsman is very similar to that of the collector or museum director to the artist. It is incumbent on each alike to pick out the very best from the abundance of what is made. That alone is mental work enough to fill a person's existence.

One must state this clearly if one is inundated, as I am, with anonymous missives which usually express the "suspicion" that a businessman whom I have recommended does not manufacture his own goods. Even if I were to see something improper about this situation—and I do not—I could not spend my time verifying the origin of goods. I am not a detective. It is a matter of indifference to me where they have come from. The main thing is that the businessman be in a position to deliver these particular goods of this particular quality. It makes no difference relative to the objects whether they are at present made in his own workshop or the work is distributed among several outside workshops. This is the only thing that concerns me here.

It is distressing to find so many ready-made, pre-tied ties in the numerous women's fashion displays. Even on men these bow ties look very ordinary. The necktie that displays a knot or a ribbon in front and is fastened in the back belongs under the rubric of paper underwear and paste diamonds. I will pass over in silence that kind of tie which is wound twice around the neck, attempting to attain its pretty effect with the aid of a piece of cardboard covered with silk fabric and some "patented" details; it is the favorite necktie of our suburban dandies. But the fact that our Viennese girls and women make use of such surrogates for the tying of a bow shows that the often celebrated Viennese chic is in the process of dying out. I wish there were a shop in Vienna whose owner would proudly be able to answer every seeker of pre-tied ties, "Pre-tied ties? No! We do not carry them!"*

*The desire for a firm that does not carry any pre-tied ties has long since been fulfilled a hundred times over! Josef Hoffmann writes in *Querschnitt*, December 1930, concerning these ties with cardboard insets which he too wore at that time and which I have criticized that they were self-tied. That is a lie. I have been wanting to lodge a complaint against this reproach of his. Hoffmann believes that I further slander Olbrich's memory by criticizing him for wearing stylish suits along with these cardboard-inset ties. This is, of course, a criticism that I cannot make of Hoffmann, even if I would want to. *1931*. [Hoffmann's comments in *Querschnitt* appear on p. 848 under the heading "Complaints." The text is as follows: "Dear Editor-in-Chief! In the last issue of *Querschnitt* . . . I read a reply by *Adolf Loos* in answer to what was in a certain sense a directly intended mockery of the excessively objective Gretor. Weeks later, he finally takes advantage of this opportunity thoroughly to slander me and my long dead friends Olbrich and Moser. If it is in fact true that Loos always wore self-tied ties, if he did not deliberately make up the story about them himself, then he must know, were his memory a little bit better, that we did the same. But his tale of the checkered frock coat with the velvet collar is surely one of his real fabrications, and has sprung from his never-dying hatred. I would gladly have kept silent if Olbrich and Moser were still alive and could defend themselves. Moser and I at one time felt the duty—since there was nothing in the whole world but copies and bad imitations of all past styles—to free ourselves from ornament and above all to begin with the simplest means so as to finally bring about a complete stylistic transformation in building. Our reasons for this may perhaps seem superfluous today, but nevertheless it must have been necessary at the time."—Ed.]

65

66

One can divide the interiors that are to be seen at our Jubilee Exhibition into three categories. The first strives to copy old furniture as faithfully as possible, the second wants to be modern, and the third seeks to modify old furniture to new needs.

Today I want to concern myself with the first category. I have already considered the second at length in my essays on the Otto Wagner room; the remaining rooms will be discussed next time. But I must pass over the third category in silence.

I believe that one can if not honor at least show enough respect to an old master to leave his works untouched. It would be a crime against the ghost of Raphael to have a copy made of the Sistine Madonna in which a Rubens-red curtain had been painted instead of a green one, and the two angels given different heads, replacing St. Sixtus and St. Barbara with St. Aloysius and St. Ursula. "But do not exaggerate," I hear the carpenter saying. "Of course, no one would do that. Raphael was a painter. But as for a piece of carpentry . . ."

But the great carpenters of the Renaissance and Baroque should be honored by their epigones in just the same way as our painters honor their old masters. That necessitates a kind of professional honor. We may paint new things and do new carpentry. We may copy old things, copy them strictly, as strictly as is possible for our time, even to the point of giving up our own personalities. But as to those who willfully violate the old, let us energetically cry, "Hands off!"

It will be objected that it is not a good idea to copy also those things which it was impossible for the old masters to do in any other way. The glass, for example, was inferior; it consists of nothing but small pieces. The great old master, if our highly developed glass industry had been available to him, would have made use of its superior products.

Certainly he would have been able to do so. But then he would also have chosen a different motif for his glass painting; then he would also have produced a different design. We have always shipwrecked ourselves on the shoals of well-intended improvements. The old figures and the old groupings are suitable only to the materials used at the time, and if one wants to work with modern glass, then one must also draw modern figures. If there is something displeasing about an old master's work, then leave him in peace. It is nothing but a delusion of grandeur to seek to improve on him.

Many people will disapprove of the fact that I am in favor of copying. Other centuries did not imitate. This practice has been reserved for our century. Copying, imitation of old forms and styles, is a result of our social conditions; these have nothing in common with the social conditions of previous centuries.

The French Revolution freed the bourgeois. Nothing could keep him from making money and from using the money however he liked. He could spend it as the nobility did, yes, or even as the king. He could ride in gold carriages, wear silk stockings, and buy castles. And why shouldn't he? It was even his duty to do so. There are people who still gravitate toward the ways of the ancien régime. Of course, they say, I now have the right to dress like the Prince of Wales. But I am not the son of the king. I am just a simple man of the bourgeoisie. No, my dear bourgeois, you do not have the right, you have the duty to dress like the Prince of Wales. Remember, you are a grandchild. Your great-grandfather and your

Furniture

Neue Freie Presse, *October 2, 1898*

65 "Chimney corner in the English style" by Sandor [Sigmund] Jaray. From Das Interieur I, *1900.*
66 Central room of a country house "in the English style." Designed by Leopold Müller and executed by J. W. Müller. From Das Interieur I, *1900.*

father fought, perhaps they shed their blood. A king and the daughter of an empress had to lay their heads on the scaffold for this idea. Now it is your turn to make the proper use of what they won by their fight.

Our bourgeoisie soon realized how the prince dressed. For clothes wear out, and when the old ones can no longer be used, new clothes are ordered. So it was now an easy thing to go to the same tailor and say to him, "Repeat!" But it was different with one's home. The high nobility and the royalty possessed such an abundance of old furniture that they were provided for for a long time, for centuries in advance. Why should they throw money out of the window purely out of a desire for novelty? On the contrary! They enjoyed the old possessions by means of which they distinguished themselves from the newly affluent bourgeoisie. For at that time, when they were still in command, the bourgeoisie did not have the means to procure things of this sort. Unused ballrooms, proper storage rooms for furniture—these it did not have. The bourgeois wore out his furniture. If he then wanted to surround himself with the selfsame things, he was forced to have copies of them made.

This is no fault. It may be typical of the parvenu, but it is the parvenu with a certain elegance. The wish to surround oneself with copies or images of old cultural artifacts that one likes when the originals are unobtainable is surely very human. The photograph of an old building, the plaster cast of a statue, the copy of a Titian would be able to recall those happy sensations that one felt on contemplating the originals.

One recalls the battle that the cabinetmaker Sandor Jaray fought with Hofrat von Scala, the director of our arts and crafts museum. But if one looks at Jaray's exhibit, one asks oneself with surprise, why all the fuss? Hofrat von Scala's basic principles have caused him to incur the antagonism of those currently in positions of power in the School of Applied Arts and the Arts and Crafts Association. The first principle, according to which everyone in all civilized countries is now working, runs as I have specified above: "Copy well, but copy *strictly*." The second runs, "In modern furniture making, English furniture is the style-setter." Both principles are energetically being battled in the camps I have named. There they still believe that it is possible to create something new in the spirit of an earlier time. They do not feel, for example, that the Gothic gas candelabrum is just as silly as the Gothic locomotive. But the second principle, obviously because the word "English" appears in it, has the effect of waving a red flag before a bull.

Let us observe how Sandor Jaray fights his battle against Herr von Scala. He exhibits a salon in the style of Louis XV, a dining room in Italian Baroque, a salon in the "Maria Theresa style," a salon in Empire—all of them authentic copies. And now comes the modern one: *horribile dictu*, an English gentleman's room. So we see that Sandor Jaray preaches the gospel of the Arts and Crafts Association, but follows Hofrat von Scala's practice.

Against Jaray the theoretician I was once forced to utter harsh words; for Jaray the practitioner I am at a loss for adequate words of praise. One may say confidently that never has a Viennese craftsman offered greater perfection in all of his pieces, in terms of both quality and quantity. Certainly the quantity is remarkable; for it is a matter of outstanding work capacity and efficiency to bring to completion, outside of his ongoing concerns, such a number of exemplary objects for a given deadline. Whatever significant decorative talents the Viennese art industry has to show for itself were called upon in the furnishing of the dining room. Anywhere one's eye happens to fall, there are no mistakes to be seen. Everything is a precise copy, strictly in the spirit of the period. And that is an art, a very significant art. For it is much easier to paint a new madonna in Raphael's "manner" than to do justice to the one in the Sistine Chapel.

Bernhard Ludwig, in addition to three modern rooms, has displayed a salon that is a copy of a room in the castle of the prince-bishop in Würzburg. The walls, ceiling, and furniture are done in green *vernis Martin*.[1] It is a charming effect, which, however, only those people can countenance who also build a red salon to go with it, in case it should be necessary—and it will be necessary—to take refuge there for a few minutes as an antidote.

J. W. Müller has displayed a gentleman's room done in German Renaissance. How homey, how solid! Its loving, able carpentry cannot easily be matched. What reverence for the ability of the old master every line, every knob displays! Nothing has been altered; even the "unbeautiful" Old German proportions, probably the most difficult trial for the sensibility of the modern man, have been retained. Rightly so. For it is a matter here of either/or. How beautiful! How glorious! The modern, capable Viennese master helping his sixteenth-century colleague to emerge victorious. What is it that Richard Wagner has his Hans Sachs say? "Honor your German masters, for thus do you conjure the good spirits." And now we know: Sandor Jaray, Bernhard Ludwig, and J. W. Müller are conjurors of the good spirits.

Furniture of the Year 1898

Neue Freie Presse, *October 9, 1898*

This kind of thing is at the exhibition too: furniture that is entirely "style-free," furniture that does not conform to any style of an earlier period. It is neither Egyptian nor Greek, neither Roman nor Gothic, neither Renaissance nor Baroque. It is apparent to anyone from the very first glance—it is furniture of the year 1898.

It is a style that will not last long. Nor should it by any means. For its authority extends only for one year. Then comes the turn of the style of 1899, which will be something completely different again. We will not really be conscious of it, but the museum directors of the next century will discover it quickly and label it correctly.

There are people who find it very regrettable that our style will not last long. They belong in China. There everything lasts for thousands of years. Others, however, know only one desire in life: always to do something better than anyone else can. Thus new forms arise of themselves.

Sandor Jaray and Müller are still sailing under foreign flags. They call their modern rooms English. And this is appropriate for Müller's charming study. One can hear voices calling this kind of thing unpatriotic. Up until now, we have imitated all nations and periods. We were content to have our carpenters work in Dutch, French, Italian, and Spanish styles. We have copied the Moors, Persians, Indians, and Chinese down to the dot over the "i" and were not a little proud of our various Japanese boudoirs. Now I ask, why in the world do we get so nervous when it comes to English rooms? What is it about the English? Why do we make an exception with them?

But J. W. Müller's room is also very noteworthy in another connection. It shows us that inexpensive materials can be used to achieve new and original effects. Opulent work is certainly a very good thing. Yet we must not forget that our crafts trade is not only for millionaires, but must concern itself with everyone else as well. Indeed, simple furniture has been produced by our top firms too in recent decades, only it was never exhibited. They acted as if they were ashamed of it. And at the Christmas Exhibition, when Hofrat von Scala also displayed simple furniture, a storm of indignation swept through our crafts world. It would be better though if this trade would establish more contact with the middle classes than it has up till now. Then the craftsmen would best be able to combat their most dangerous enemy: imitation. For the glazier who cuts plain and colorless windows is not the foe of the glass painter; it is rather the manufacturer of translucent paper who is. And it is not the carpenter who produces plain furniture who is the enemy of the wood sculptor, but rather the sawdust-and-glue ornament presser.

Sandor Jaray's English room is not English. A Persian carpet in a room still does not make it a Persian room. A Japanese screen and a few knickknacks to go with it still do not make a room Japanese. A lady of the old English aristocracy whom I accompanied to the Jaray exhibit recognized all of the stylistic periods immediately: "This is Louis XVI, this Italian, this Rococo, this Empire! But what is that?" "That is English," I answered.

The room is certainly not English. However, that is no defect. It is Viennese. Everything exudes amiability and elegance. It only seems so English to us because a great number of English forms are used in it. This is to be welcomed. We must put to good use all inspirations that come from outside. The masters of the

German Renaissance did so too. Only let's allow the dead to rest in peace.

The pride and centerpiece of Bernhard Ludwig's exhibit is the dining room. It is a room that will begin a new era in the Viennese furniture industry. What makes this room so significant? It's the fact that the greatest wood ornament sculptor of our time has given it its decoration.

It is a remarkable room, the birthplace, as it were, of this wood carver. Before the creation of this room, no one, not even he himself, knew what he was capable of. When Bernhard Ludwig conceived of the plan to do a dining room of oak with wood carvings—this was six weeks before the opening of the exhibition—he was not yet aware of the scope of his undertaking. The sculptor—Franz Zelezny is his name—was well known to him as a capable man. Zelezny had the reputation prior to then of delivering the best and most stylistically pure work. But Bernhard Ludwig wanted something else. He did only what was strictly carpentry work and left the space for the ornament blank. "Here, my dear Zelezny, put something together over here for me." "In what style?" "In your style!"

In his style! How that went to the man's heart and soul. In his own style, just as he had always imagined, dreamed, and fancied during those times that he, the artist, had had to transform the philistine sketches of the furniture designer into form. Then he might attain his desire after all! And he began. At first with trepidation, not entirely trusting his own raw power, but then step by step more strongly and freely. What was Gothic? What was Rococo? Here is nature, now go to it!

"Here is nature, now stylize" is what is taught in the school. Oh, these "stylizing" arts and crafts professors! One of them publishes a work with stylized plants and animals. If you ask him for which material all of these things are stylized, you get as an answer, "Of course, you can use them entirely as you please."

67 Wood-carved sideboard door by Franz Zelezny. From Das Interieur IV, *1903.*

Clearly this is nonsense. Stylization in this sense taught by the drawing teachers does not exist. The drawing teacher is, of course, able to stylize, but only on the drawing board, on the planar surface. He is able to produce an animal, a plant, or an object two-dimensionally. Naturally it is not easy. He must make lines which do not exist in nature; other lines which are there he must leave out. Nevertheless he can—especially when he uses brush and canvas and becomes a painter—approach nature very closely.

Every artisan, every artist wants to be able to do this. The stonemason of the Middle Ages caught himself a salamander. "Just you wait, fellow, I'll carve you in stone. As a gargoyle." And he began to carve away. Then he said to his comrade the painter, "Look here, brother painter, see what a fine portrait I have made. Is it not the living image of the salamander?"

His comrade the painter shook his head. As far as seeing went, he had had more experience. That is quite easy to understand. Whereas the stonemason used his eyes to make comparisons to nature only rarely, it was he, the painter, who racked his brains to wring a new ground plan out of the stonemason's foundations, or to invent a new quatrefoil strictly according to the rules. It was he whom the Rochlitz Secession had set to thinking, the secession of that unfaithful brotherhood that had rebelled against the old stonemasonry customs.[1] For his whole lifetime, the painter had had only one task to reflect upon: how he could penetrate the secret forms of nature, the forms which everyone saw but no one was able to put on paper.

So the painter shook his head. "But dear brother stonemason," he said, "you are gravely deluding yourself if you believe that your work has even the slightest resemblance to the animal. Look at the front legs! They are much too long. And the neck here, and here, and here . . ."

The stonemason became angry. "Well, how am I supposed to support the animal on the phiale if I do not make his front legs a little longer!" For everything he had an excuse, and on everything he faulted the painter. He was completely right. For he saw it thus, and so that was the way it was.

Just think of it. The man had worked in the mason's hut twelve hours a day since he was fourteen. No wonder he saw the world differently from the painter. When one has worked in stone for his entire lifetime, he begins to think stones and to see stones. The man had an eye of stone that turned all things into stone. He had developed a hand of stone, and this hand of itself transformed all things into stone. Under his gaze and hand, the acanthus leaf and the grape leaf acquired a different appearance than they would have under the gaze and hand of a goldsmith. For the latter sees everything in gold. And the higher a master mason climbs, the more he loses whatever clings to him of the workshop. He comes closer and closer to nature until he has finally overcome the workshop. The blades of grass, ferns, beetles, butterflies, and lizards on the Rothschild centerpieces by Wenzel Jamnitzer[2] are like casts made from nature. And so the work of the artisan and the artist represents a great battle between materials and nature. But the drawing teacher teaches, "The main thing is stylization. I will lecture on rules for stylization in the next class."

Zelezny has not stylized. He is the master in whose gaze everything forms itself into wood, in whose hand everything is given shape in wood; he is an artist who does not first mangle his flowers and leaves on the drawing board. He creates directly in the wood, and for this reason his ornaments acquire that freshness and self-assurance characteristic of all works of genius. It is not the slave work of the ancients, who had the capacity to produce one and the same kind of ornamental molding, whether astragal or ovolo, by the mile. It is the work of the free worker at the end of the nineteenth century who creates out of joy in his own work, and creates quickly and abundantly.

Here is a chair. This chair is a product of art. If I paint a picture of the chair, then the painted chair is only an image of this product of art, hence a secondhand work of art.

Let us attempt to apply the same thing to letters. Letters can be chiseled in stone, cast in bronze, written with the pen. These stone and bronze letters can be put on paper with the help of light and shadow and perspective. These are, however, only images of letters and not the letters themselves. The letters on the paper have no other dimension than that of the printer's ink.

There are carpenters who delight in making furniture that is only good as display models. Likewise, there are also printers who pride themselves on creating images of written, chiseled, and cast words. Types are chosen that cast magnificent shadows. Then the whole thing is set into relief so that it appears to have been typeset upon a board; this effect is evoked by shadow lines to the right of the letters and underneath. But they are not satisfied with this. They even attempt to imitate printing itself. They do so by letting a piece of paper look like it has a pin fastened to it, or is torn, or else has one corner folded down. Here is simulated an obliquely placed card, so that in perspective the letters have to become smaller and smaller; there one such fake sheet of paper even casts a shadow on the real paper! All this always secondhand!

But the proper book printer does not want to imitate printed works; he would rather be the creator of new works himself. Thus when we speak of the work of printers, we are, of course, only referring to those new creations by talented individuals. But it must not be kept a secret that there are even *typefaces* that imitate drawn, lithographed, and written letters. This belongs to the chapter on imitation.

Recently the great popularity of the poster posed a new problem for artists. It concerned the solving of the difficult problem of how letters, proper printer's letters, could be unified with images in such a way that the two together would result in a perfect work of art.

This was not an easy task. The unification of two different graphic techniques is impossible. Imagine, for example, the effect on a mountain landscape that is evoked with oil colors in the customary way if, in the middle of the blue sky or the green lake, the words "Alpine herbal wine is the best!" were inset in the usual printer's type. In fact, it is not even necessary to imagine it, for it can be seen frequently enough.

So the problem was now to join letters to pictorial representation. This was easy for the lithographers. Chéret, the lithographer, had already taught them how to draw lithographed figures.[1] But this did not take care of the book printers. The man destined to create something new and unprecedented could only be a book printer. He had to be able to think only in the black ink of the printer; the whole world had to appear to him like a large piece of paper on which God above had printed man and beast, courtyard and house, tree and mountain, sky and stone. It had to be someone who, without pondering or brooding, completely naively and out of an innermost impulse, could create "printed" people, people out of black printer's ink, people whom one could never imagine leaving the paper they were on, people of whom one would never demand to know how they looked from the side or behind. How would the drawing teacher say it? "Stylized men."

Neue Freie Presse, *October 23, 1898*

68 An example of Will H. Bradley's Colonial-style typography of 1896. From The American Handbook of Printing, *New York, 1913.*

69

69 *Advertisement for the printing firm of Angerer & Göschl. From* Kunst und Kunsthandwerk, *no. 1, 1898.*

70 *Page from* Die Wiener Werkstätte 1903-1928: Modernes Kunstgewerbe und Sein Weg, *Vienna, 1929, illustrating Josef Hoffmann's "much controversed knives, spoons, and forks."*

71 *A right-hand page from* Die Wiener Werkstätte 1903-1928. *Outside margin is one-eighth inch.*

72 *Page from* Die Wiener Werkstätte 1903-1928, *with an inscription from Peter Altenberg to Josef Hoffmann. It reads, "Friendship, friendship, you so often abused and slandered word, you are nothing but the 'recognition of a just mind' tempered 'by the good will of the gentle heart'!"*

Such a book printer appeared. It was Bradley, the American, who now lives in Springfield, Massachusetts.[2] He is the prototype of the proud, stubborn typesetter who does not allow pieces of art done by the draftsman to appear with his printed letters. With him there is no nonsense, no types that rank above the others. His letters never jump around. There is strict supervision all the time in the printing shop to make sure that the letters form a mathematically straight line. This is an established rule. He knows nothing of aerial perspectives, of changes in shades of color within a single color field as the distance increases. Here one color ends; here the next begins. His vision is very primitive. He sees only two colors and colorlessness, which for him means white paper. For he must make do with two "book printer's colors." But with these two shades he creates more powerful effects than do our painters with their nine-color printing. His world is small, small as the world of handicrafts has always been. But in this world he is king.

Our Viennese printers have no desire for power. They have allowed the painter and the architect to snatch the scepter from their hands, and these men naturally manage to use it in their own way. The latter cannot do book printer's work, though, just as the painter who can paint a picture of a shoe perfectly well can never make one. For believe me, the work of the shoemaker is just as difficult or as easy to learn as any of the other crafts. The only reason that painters do not yet make shoes for us—since pretty soon they will have taken over *all* of the workshops—is that our feet are more sensitive than our eyes. Our eyes put up with a great deal.

It has not always been this way. When men had more sensitive eyes, they also demanded that they not be annoyed by inferior print and inferior paper while they were reading and thinking. Books were given the proper width of white paper on the right, left, and underneath, so that there was adequate space for the fingers to grip the book. Today one has to put his fingers into the middle of the print.*

People who demand everything from a good book that can be demanded from one will seldom do well around us. This is all the more regrettable since the technical capacity of the Viennese firms in the area of graphics is unparalleled in Europe. Where in the world is there a firm like Angerer & Göschl, whose importance we first hear of abroad? We have simply become too accustomed to it.

Among the various printers, the firm of Adolph Holzhausen stands out. They only print scholarly works, though, thereby easily circumventing the many difficulties posed by the belles lettres. For it is remarkable: nearly all the scholarly works represent themselves in a very sound and elegant fashion, while the more literary works have to submit to all possible disfigurations.

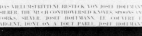
DAS VIELUMSTRITTENE BESTECK VON JOSEF HOFFMANN
SILBER. THE MUCH-CONTROVERSED KNIVES, SPOONS AND
FORKS, SILVER. JOSEF HOFFMANN. LE COUVERT EN
ARGENT, DONT ON A TOUT PARLE. JOSEF HOFFMANN

70

DAS BUCH DES NEUEN KUNSTGEWERBES
Nach Josef Hoffmanns Anregung und ihrer Verwirklichung durch Mathilde Flögl ist in diesem Buche der Netzdruck als unentbehrlicher Vermittler des gegenstandtreuen Lichtbildes in den festlichen Rahmen prunkfarbiger, von Blatt zu Blatt wechselnder Flächenteilungen gesetzt. Eine buchkünstlerische Neuerung, welche ebenso wie die farbige Reliefpressung des Einbandes kaum jemalsvorher in gleicher Folgerichtigkeit angewendet worden ist. Es war nicht möglich, Werke aller Künstler der Wiener Werkstätte, deren Archiv mehr als 17.000 Entwürfe enthält, aufzunehmen. Nicht einmal alle Zweige der hier geübten Erzeugungsarten konnten berücksichtigt werden. Die Auswahl soll die freiwillig übernommene und opfervolle Mission der Wiener Werkstätte erweisen: das durch die Persönlichkeitswerte ihres Urhebers bereicherte Kunstgewerbe zu pflegen, um so der mißverständlichen und seelenlosen Nachahmung, der verflachenden Mechanisierung und Merkantilisierung der zeiteigenen Produktion einen Damm zu setzen. Wie der stets zunehmende Einfluß der Wiener Werkstätte auf die Produktion der zivilisierten Welt zeigt, erweisen sich noch immer Kunst und Kunsthandwerk am wirksamsten für die Annäherung der Völker. William Morris hatte es erkannt, als er mit einer die gesamte Welt umspannenden Gebärde darauf hinwies: »Alle Völker fühlten diese Kunst; von Bokhara bis Galway, von Island bis Madras schimmerte die ganze Welt in ihrem Glanz und schauerte unter ihrer Kraft. Sie riß die Scheidewände zwischen Religionen und Rassen nieder. Sie erfreute Christen und Muselmänner, Kelten, Teutonen und Römer und brachte sie gemeinschaftlich in die Höhe. Perser, Tartaren und Araber reichten einander ihre Gaben und nahmen sie voneinander an.«

71

…cache. Et dans l'histoire de l'architecture contemporaine, dans la marche vers une esthétique contemporaine, le Prof. Hoffmann, occupe l'une des places les plus lumineuses.

72

*Today, in 1931, we are already much further advanced! Everywhere books are printed with a wide white margin on the inside next to the binding. This is completely nonsensical. On the outside, the letters continue all the way to the edge; even the pictures are there. One cannot see them because one is forced to cover them with one's thumbs. A united front exists in this matter, from the Constructivists to the Wiener Werkstätte. See, for example, the Werkstätte Jubilee edition of 1928! There is a great deal to say about this Jubilee edition; the verdict on this piece of work speaks for itself. I will only say this much here:
1. The style of the ornament is stolen from Sonja Delauney [*sic*], whom I greatly respect. It was invented for printed silk and (in accordance with my thesis that a thing will continue to be of aesthetic value as long as it continues to be of physical value) is very much appropriate in that context.
2. Instead of the cutlery by Josef Hoffmann which I have presented and criticized in all my lectures to the general amusement of my audience, a more correct and normal table setting is depicted in the book. The caption reads, "This is what the much-criticized cutlery of the Wiener Werkstätte looks like!"
3. The quotations from Peter Altenberg could create the impression that P. A. was an admirer of the Wiener Werkstätte. Perhaps that is their intention. However, one can read from his works that he was the greatest and most honest enemy of the Wiener Werkstätte.
1931.

Additional Essays
1897-1900

*73 A small workroom in Goldman &
Salatsch menswear store, Adolf Loos,
1898. From* Das Interieur II, *1901.*

School Exhibition of the School of Applied Arts

Die Zeit, *October 30, 1897*

The school of the Austrian Museum, our School of Applied Arts, has had on exhibit since the ninth of this month the work of the preceding school year. One sees the usual objects executed with the usual precision; the usual applause resounds in the daily newspapers. And truly, even the most critical observer upon viewing the contents of Ferstel's solid Italian rooms—the still-lives, the flower pieces, the nudes, the pictures of saints, the Tadema-like[1] scenes, the portraits, the statues, the reliefs, the woodcuts, the drawings for furniture journals, and all the rest—has to say, "How *much* has been done here!"

Painting, sculpture, and graphic arts have a kind of second-class academy at the school on the Stubenring. They are competing with our Art College on the Schillerplatz, and even if the latter's work cannot be matched because of the short period of study, nevertheless much is achieved in this noble contest. On the Schillerplatz, they come to the realization more quickly that it is necessary to wake up out of their lethargy. On the Stubenring, they merely produce second-rate artists.

Perhaps you think that no one ought to raise any objections. That is wrong. For this competition takes place at the expense of something. It is the trades, the handicrafts.

Let us say it straight out: the arts and crafts are simply being cheated by this kind of behavior. The small sum allotted by the budget of the Ministry of Education to arts and crafts instruction is totally wasted on this purpose. We Austrians, who were supposed to conduct ourselves in this connection with the strictest economy because of the lack of funds, are letting our crafts hunger and starve at the expense of "great art."

This crime has been committed for decades without an advocate having been found for the wronged party, the crafts. It is no longer any secret to our tradesmen: the work force that issues forth from this institution is of no use to the workshop, to life, or to the public. Crammed full of false ideas, without familiarity with materials, without any sensitivity to what is elegant and progressive, without knowledge of contemporary tendencies, they either add to the great number of insignificant painters and sculptors, or make up abroad for their lack of training here—if they possess enough capacity to adapt to foreign circumstances. Then they are simply lost to us. We cannot bring them into the school ourselves; we lack the strength to do so. On the contrary! We expect even that such an institution should give us the impetus to get moving.

We have been standing still for a long time and we continue to stand still. In matters of arts and crafts, the whole world has been marching forward courageously during the last decade under the leadership of the English. The distance between us and the others grows ever greater, and if we do not want to lose the opportunity to join up with them, the moment has arrived. Even Germany has accelerated its pace from behind and will soon catch up with the procession. What new life there is abroad! Painters, sculptors, and architects are leaving their comfortable studios; they are putting their precious art on the shelf and taking up their positions at the anvil, at the weaver's loom, at the drawing board, in front of the kiln, at the joiner's bench! Away with all the doodling, the paper art! Now it's time to extract new forms and new lines from life, from customs, from comfort, from utility! Onward and upward, comrades, art is something that must be conquered!

In view of this ever-growing enthusiasm for the honest crafts movement, it is with profound regret that we see our young artists standing to one side, half indifferent. Even those who might be summoned are flirting, as we have seen, with the fine arts. The reverse—the return of the artists to the crafts—is certainly not the case at all. Is there really so little capacity for enthusiasm left in young people?

From the few handicraft works at the exhibition we can already answer this question. It is as if the student's very soul had been forced out of his body onto the drawing paper, corrected, constructed, modeled, and taught, all for the sake of a rigid dogma. Nature is studied—but without consequence. Such study is surely only a means to an end for the arts and crafts. The goal that is supposed to be attained is the ability to stylize that which exists in nature, or better, to make nature serve the material out of which it is to be modeled. But the courage, the strength, and, above all, the knowledge of the material necessary for this are lacking in the school. The dogma that is going to destroy this school is the view that our crafts must be reformed from above, from the ateliers down. But revolutions always come from below. And this "below" is the workshop.

The view still prevails here that the designing of a chair may be entrusted only to someone who knows the five columnar orders inside and out. I believe, however, that before all else such a person must understand something about the activity of sitting. For there is surely nothing in the order of a column from which one can benefit in designing a chair. Model draftsmen, who do outstanding work for publications—an activity which must, of course, be considered as belonging to graphic art—fail completely when it comes to producing their own designs. Lack of understanding for the material with respect to the details from nature (one has only to look at the uncarpenter-like profiles) and tedious copying (the professionals call it *spranzen*) in the decorative drawings of interior spaces are the common features of all three specialized ateliers at our school.

Individual teachers cannot be reproached for this. It is the spirit of guilt hovering over the entire institution that is at fault.

When it comes to speaking of the decorative painting, one need only repeat what has already been said. Here too there is skillful work—as long as the painting speaks for itself alone. For the craft trades, however, the best drawings are worthless. Naturalistically drawn pumpkins—to pick out one example—with meticulous shadows that render them remarkably three-dimensional are not enough. Especially when they are intended for a tapestry frieze on the wall just below the ceiling. In such an unfortunate room one would not dare to tread heavily. After all, one of the pumpkins might fall on one's head! It is the maintenance of such illusions which is guaranteed by skillful drawing. We could go through each and every sheet of paper in this way, but the one example is really sufficient to testify to the empty-headedness of the draftsman who sees only as far as the end of the drawing board.

We may hope that this is the last of this sort of exhibition. The arts and crafts will finally be given what is theirs. A new spirit has moved into the museum with the arrival of the new director, Hofrat von Scala. Let us hope that this spirit will be strong and relentless enough toward the old to act effectively as the master of the house. The Austrian crafts are looking forward to this.

74

75

It cannot be denied: the collection of copies of old furniture now to be seen at the Austrian Museum has created a sensation. It is the talk of the town. One would think he had been transported back into the golden age of the Austrian arts and crafts. Those were the days when Vienna ranked first in the art of handicrafts, when the unforgettable Eitelberger[1] was still at the helm in the Stubenring and the public interest could hardly have been greater. Now once again one reads reports in the daily papers about the new directions and trends; people debate; people argue. And what is more, people are again attending the Christmas Exhibition.

Now what has actually happened? The Austrian Museum has acquired a new director, and this new director has opened up a new terrain for us. Some say that he has made way for the modern style. Others say that he has introduced Anglicism. A third group says that he emphasizes the practical aspect of utilitarian objects. Who is correct? Actually all of them. But they have not expressed it correctly. He has, if I may say so, discovered the bourgeois household.

I know that this explanation will occasion a general shaking of heads. Have we not assembled, preserved in the museum, and studied the best objects of all periods and all classes and stations of society? Have we not used and imitated the best bourgeois pieces of the Gothic, the Renaissance, the Baroque, and the Empire? Have we not always furnished our houses in the bourgeois style?

No, we have not. Our wives and daughters slept in beds just like the one in the Trianon where that unfortunate emperor's daughter, Marie Antoinette, dreamt of splendor, happiness, and luxury. The head butcher, that fine sir, gazed with pride at his Old German sofa, its motifs taken from the wainscoted walls of the state room in the town hall of Bremen; it was fashioned into a combination of a little piece of that room—the whole wainscoting would have been too expensive—and a cushioned chest. And the guests of a well-to-do gentleman of the stock exchange loll about in armchairs that look very much like the one from which Napoleon once dictated his laws to the world. It is not even permissible for the imperial "N" to be lacking. And yet that Corsican used this throne only once; the rest of the time he and his guests contented themselves with less pretentious furniture.

But why are we so unfamiliar with the real bourgeois household? Because relatively little of it has come down to us. For the bourgeois citizen wore out his furniture; he used it daily, and in the end he lit his fire with it. He had no money for luxurious and splendid rooms. And if one or the other piece happened to be preserved, there was seldom a museum that would grant asylum to the old domestic war-horse.

The piece did not exactly distinguish itself by its artistic workmanship. And even if here or there one of the pieces did win itself a modest little place in a collection, it was certainly overlooked. The situation was completely different with the furniture of princes. It was never or hardly ever used, and it asserted its elegant, indolent character in the fact that it displayed motifs of high architecture and was provided with abundant ornamention. But even if it was unfit for practical use, it was nevertheless not without purpose. Its purpose was to represent and bear witness to the wealth, the splendor, the love of art, and the taste of its owner. The furniture of princes thus undoubtedly was preserved for good reason and constitutes the pride and joy of every museum.

The Christmas Exhibition at the Austrian Museum

The Bourgeois Household: The Lefler Room

Die Zeit, *December 18, 1897*

74 The "Lefler Room." Heinrich Lefler, Hans Rathausky, Franz Schönthaler, Jr., Josef Urban. Winter Exhibition, Austrian Museum for Art and Industry, Vienna, 1898. From Kunst und Kunsthandwerk, *no. 1, 1898. 75 "Lefler Room."*

The nineteenth century misused these exhibition objects by taking them as practical models. The barriers erected by the royalty against the high nobility, and by the high nobility against the lower nobility, and by the lower nobility against the bourgeoisie, had collapsed, and everyone could furnish his home and dress according to his own taste. Thus it can really be no surprise to us that every house servant wanted to furnish his home like those in the court, and every waiter wanted to dress like the Prince of Wales. It would be wrong, however, to see progress in this situation. For princely furniture, the result of an immense superabundance of wealth, cost great sums of money. But since this kind of wealth was not available to the general public, they therefore copied at the expense of materials and execution. As a result, superficiality, hollowness, and that horrible monster, imitation, which threatens to suck the marrow out of the bones of our crafts, have made their entry.

The lives that we lead, moreover, are in conflict with the objects with which we surround ourselves. We forget that one must have a living room in addition to a throne room. We calmly allow ourselves to be maltreated by our stylish furniture. We give ourselves bruises on our knees, and we sit down with ornaments at our backs and under our behinds. We have gotten Renaissance, Baroque, and Rococo blisters one after the other in the last two decades from the various ornamented handles of our vessels. But we have not grumbled, for those who resisted would have been pilloried as imbeciles and people lacking in any higher understanding of art.

But what I am bringing up here applies only to the Continent. Over there, on the other side of the English Channel, lives a race of free citizens that has long ago been weaned from the old restrictions. Parvenu impulses no longer find any fertile ground there. The English forswore princely luxury and princely splendor in their homes. Clothing regulations were not known for ages and thus no particular satisfaction was taken in imitating the great men of past ages. Most important to them was their own comfort. And under the influence of this kind of bourgeoisie, even the nobility of that country slowly underwent a change. It became simple and unpretentious.

A nation that produces such a self-assured and independent bourgeoisie is destined soon to bring the bourgeois style in the home to its fullest flower. The best workers can be employed in this pursuit; they can concentrate their energies on this task. Meanwhile, in other countries, it is the first-rate craftsmen who assume the responsibility for the furniture of the princes, and the furniture of the bourgeois household is produced by the second-rate workers. One has only to observe the two most famous designers in England and France of the same epoch. Let us take as an example Thomas Chippendale and Meissonier, the *dessinateur* of Louis XV. Among the work of the latter we find only designs for the king's state rooms and banquet halls, while with Chippendale, the unassuming title of his book of engravings is already characteristic: *The Gentleman and Cabinetmaker's Director, Being a Collection of Designes of Household Furniture.*

It is thus easy to see that in any collection of bourgeois furniture the lion's share is bound to fall to the English. They have even given a home to many pieces of German bourgeois furniture which have long since been forgotten here and which are now making their way back to us by way of England. There are some interesting examples of this. Let me mention one here: the bright red lacquered chair with yellow wickerwork that seems so terribly English to us today (strutting chairs or hen roosts, we call them disdainfully) can be found in numerous pic-

76

77

76 *Ash and walnut armchair by*
Thomas Chippendale, 1740. From
Kunst und Kunsthandwerk, *no. 1,*
1898.
77 *Mahogany armchair with cane*
seat and back, English, 1660. From
Kunst und Kunsthandwerk, *no. 1,*
1898.

tures of German interiors from the eighteenth century, especially those by Chodowiecki.[2]

Yet another circumstance accounts for the great number of English designs. England also was the first nation to take up the battle against imitation. Now we too are slowly beginning to marshal our forces against it. Imitation jewelry and false furs are, thank God, no longer considered fashionable around here. And we must be grateful to our Christmas Exhibition for inspiring us to apply this new doctrine to our home furnishings as well. Let whoever does not have the money for a stamped-leather chair simply make do with a straw chair. Many a person will be appalled at the thought. A straw chair, how ordinary! Go on, my dear Viennese, a straw seat is only as ordinary as not having any diamonds or as having a simple cloth collar on a winter coat. Only imitation jewelry, fur collars, and leather chairs are ordinary.

Thus, the realization is making its way to us too that we must place the main emphasis on the solid and the practical, especially when money is not sufficient for the elaborate and the decorative. Painted inlays, woodcuts made of compressed sawdust and glue, "botch-up-your-home" windows and other authorized items from the arsenal of imitation, doors and windows painted to simulate hardwood are slowly disappearing from the bourgeois home. Bourgeois pride has awakened; the doctrine of the parvenu is out of fashion.

The clincher of this exhibition is an interior, a collaborative work by the Viennese painter Heinrich Lefler, the sculptor Hans Rathausky, and the architects Franz Schönthaler, Jr., and Josef Urban. Around town it is simply called "the Lefler Room." This abbreviated name has become absolutely necessary since in recent weeks it has been on the tip of everyone's tongue. Rejoiced over by the young, despised by the old, this room has the significance of the first stirring on Viennese soil of the modern spirit in the applied arts.

To be sure, it looks modern. But if one looks a little closer, it is only our good old German Renaissance *gschnaszimmer*[3] seen in a modern light. Nothing is missing. The wood inlay with its intarsia work stenciled in, the Old German ornamental divan (God bless it!) from which the tin lions' heads that were nailed on were always torn off (they had played the very necessary and difficult role of holding the Persian slipcover on), and whose mugs and Old German pitchers rattled around so beautifully whenever one made the slightest movement—everything, everything about it has been appropriated. Only it has been disguised so well that at first one does not recognize it at all. Whereas, for example, an Old German pitcher could have fallen from the old ornamental divan onto your head, now English vases fall down, and that's for sure. This is a great advance if one considers that thereby, as it were, indecision is avoided and the pottery trade benefits by the heavy rate of breakage.

We see already in which direction this room is tending. It brings us modern forms in the old spirit. Thus one has no right to speak of a modern room. The correct thing would have been to make use of old forms in the new spirit.

Let us pass over to the individual works. Lefler produced charming wallpaper that is by far the best in the whole room. Our Austrian wallpaper industry has nothing else like it to show for itself. Just think: a modern wallpaper that has nothing English about it and whose Viennese origin is apparent from the first glance. The appliqué cushions and the carpets are also outstanding. The "Drag-

78 "Sleeping Beauty" ornamental glass window in the Lefler Room. From Kunst und Kunsthandwerk, no. 1, 1898.

93

on Battle" mohair carpet betrays a solid mastery of the technique. But Lefler's technique already faltered with the design of the glass windows. He produced two of them, the one "Cinderella," the other "Sleeping Beauty." Both of them betray a wavering between two techniques, glass painting and the American work with glass enameling. "Cinderella" still achieves a harmonious effect since here glass painting was employed only in such places as it was absolutely necessary, in the faces, for example. But "Sleeping Beauty" is unpardonable. The painted hedge of roses is a blow to all honest glasswork. With what joy the glassworker would have seized the opportunity to display his technique on the roses! For every leaf a different enameled glazing! These roses cry out for the American technique, all the more so as something close to this appears at less important points. It is for this reason that the window produces such an unharmonious effect. The attempt, however, to leave the middle window free for the undisturbed view of the outside seems to me worthy of imitation. All in all Lefler's work displays a fresh straightforwardness and a decisive ability to make use of new techniques.

This cannot be said of the other works in the exhibition. They only imitate inlay in the wainscoting of the walls; the banal wallpaper work on the ceiling persuades one of a lack of true elegance. A superb wooden chest is ruined by the artificially patined bronze relief, which, if it were real, would not give its owner good marks for cleanliness. Bear in mind that the green patina that has built up on bronze objects buried in the damp earth for thousands of years was altogether absent so long as they were still in use. One could at least expect our moderns to be opposed to this sham! I have already spoken at the outset about the shelfboard that functions as the crown of the carelessly worked sofa. Even the clock, on which it is impossible to read the time, is strained. In earlier days it was impossible to read because the clock face was "stylish"; now it is impossible because the clock face is square.

Thus it would be incorrect to characterize this room as modern. The modern spirit requires above all else that the utilitarian object be practical. It holds beauty to mean the highest perfection. And since the impractical never is perfect, it can also never be beautiful. After all, the modern spirit demands absolute truth. I have already said above that imitation and pseudo-elegance are finally, thank God, becoming unmodern. And thirdly the modern spirit demands individuality. That means, in general, that the king furnishes his home like a king, the bourgeois like a bourgeois, and the peasant like a peasant; and in particular, that every king, every bourgeois, and every peasant expresses his own characteristic qualities in the furnishing of his home. It is the task of modern artists to raise the taste of the multitude in its various characteristic class gradations; in doing so they are fulfilling the needs of the intellectual aristocracy at any given time. Have our four artists done this? Does their ladies' chamber correspond to the elegance of the aristocratic lady? No. Nor does it correspond to the elegance of the manufacturer's wife, nor in any way to the elegance of the wife of the bourgeois. It corresponds only to the elegance of the coquette.

Who does not know of Potemkin's villages, the ones that Catherine's cunning favorite built in the Ukraine?[1] They were villages of canvas and pasteboard, villages intended to transform a visual desert into a flowering landscape for the eyes of Her Imperial Majesty. But was it a whole city which that cunning minister was supposed to have produced?

Surely such things are only possible in Russia!

But the Potemkin city of which I wish to speak here is none other than our dear Vienna herself. It is a hard accusation; it will also be hard for me to succeed in proving it. For to do so I need listeners with a very fine sense of justice, such listeners, unfortunately, as are scarcely to be found in our city nowadays.

Anyone who tries to pass himself off as something better than he is is a swindler; he deserves to be held in general contempt, even if no one has been harmed by him. But if someone attempts to achieve this effect with false jewels and other imitations? There are countries where such a man would suffer the same fate. But in Vienna we have not yet come so far. There is only a small circle of people who would feel that in such a case an immoral act has occurred, that they have been swindled. But today it is not only by means of the fake watch chain, not only by the furnishings of one's residence (which consist of outright imitations), but also by one's residence itself, the building in which one lives, that everyone wants to make himself out to be something more than he is.

Whenever I stroll along the Ring, it always seems to me as if a modern Potemkin had wanted to carry out his orders here, as if he had wanted to persuade somebody that in coming to Vienna he had been transported into a city of nothing but aristocrats.

Whatever the Italy of the Renaissance produced in the way of lordly palaces was plundered in order to conjure up as if by magic a new Vienna for Her Majesty the Mob. A new Vienna where only those people lived who could afford to occupy an entire palace from socle to cornice line. On the ground floor were the stables; on the low-ceilinged, intermediate mezzanine level were the servants; on the first of the upper stories, with its rich and elaborate architecture, were the banquet and ceremonial rooms; above them were the residential and sleeping quarters. The Viennese landlord very much enjoyed owning such a palace; the tenant also enjoyed living in one. The simple man, who had rented only one room and a w.c. on the uppermost floor, was overcome with a blissful feeling of feudal splendor and lordly grandeur whenever he looked at the building he lived in from the outside. Does the owner of an imitation diamond not gaze fondly at the glittering glass? Oh, the tale of the deceiver deceived!

It will be objected that I impute false intentions to the Viennese. It is the architects who are at fault; the architects should not have built this way. I must defend the architects. For every city gets the architects it deserves. Supply and demand regulate architectural form. He whose work most accords with the wishes of the populace will have the most to build. And the most capable architect may depart from this life without ever having received a commission. The others, however, create schools of followers. Then one builds in a certain way because he has become accustomed to it. And he must build this way. The building speculator would most dearly like to have his facades entirely plastered from top to bottom. It costs the least. And at the same time, he would be acting in the truest, most correct, and most artistic way. But people would not want to

Potemkin City

Ver Sacrum, *July 1898*

79 Caricature from Figaro: Wiener Luft, *depicting "the passing afternoon parade on the Kärntnerring." 1883.*

95

move into the building. And so, in the interest of rentability, the landlord is forced to nail on a particular kind of facade, and only this kind.

Yes, literally nail on! For these Renaissance and Baroque palaces are not actually made out of the material of which they seem. Some pretend that they are made of stone, like the Roman and Tuscan palaces; others of stucco, like the buildings of the Viennese Baroque. But they are neither. Their ornamental details, their corbels, festoons, cartouches, and denticulation, are nailed-on poured cement. Of course, this technique too, which comes into use for the first time in this century, is perfectly legitimate. But it does not do to use it with forms whose origin is intimately bound up with a specific material simply because no technical difficulties stand in the way. It would have been the artist's task to find a new formal language for new materials. Everything else is imitation.

But this was not even a matter of concern to the Viennese of the last architectural epoch. He was delighted, in fact, to be able to imitate with such lowly materials the more expensive material that served as the model. Like the authentic parvenu that he was, he believed that the others would not notice the deception. That is what the parvenu always thinks. At first he is sure that the false shirt dickeys, the false fur collars, all of the imitation objects with which he surrounds himself fulfill their roles perfectly. It is only those who stand above him, those who have already surmounted the parvenu stage and are among the initiated, who smile at his futile exertions. And in time the parvenu's eyes too open up. First he recognizes one inauthenticity among his friends, then another, in things he had earlier thought were authentic. Then, resigned, he gives them up for himself as well.

80 View of the north side of the Kärntnerring, Vienna, as it appeared in 1873. Wood engraving by F. W. Bader, after a drawing by L. E. Petrovits.
81 View of the south side of the Kärntnerring, Vienna, as it appeared in 1873. Wood engraving by F. W. Bader, after a drawing by L. E. Petrovits.

Poverty is no disgrace. Not everyone can come into the world the lord of a feudal estate. But to pretend to one's fellow men that one has such an estate is ridiculous and immoral. After all, should we be ashamed to live in a rental apartment in a building with many others who are our social equals? Should we be ashamed of the fact that there are materials that are too expensive for us to build with? Should we be ashamed to be nineteenth-century men and not men who want to live in a building whose architectural style belongs to an earlier age? If we ceased to be ashamed, you would see how quickly we would acquire an architecture suited to our own times. This is what we have anyway, you will object. But I mean an architectural style that we will be able to pass on to posterity in good conscience, an architectural style that even in the distant future will be pointed to with pride. But we have not yet found this architectural style in our century in Vienna.

Whether one tries to create out of canvas, pasteboard, and paint the wood huts where happy peasants dwell, or to erect out of brick and poured cement would-be stone palaces where feudal lords seem to reside, it is the same in principle. Potemkin's spirit has hovered over Viennese architecture in this century.

80

81

Ladies' fashion! You disgraceful chapter in the history of civilization! You tell of mankind's secret desires. Whenever we peruse your pages, our souls shudder at the frightful aberrations and scandalous depravities. We hear the whimpering of abused children, the shrieks of maltreated wives, the dreadful outcry of tortured men, and the howls of those who have died at the stake. Whips crack, and the air takes on the burnt smell of scorched human flesh. *La bête humaine . . .*

No, man is not a beast. Beasts love; they love simply and according to the ordering of nature. But man misuses his own nature and through it, his own eros. We are beasts that have been penned up in stables, beasts from whom natural nourishment has been withheld, beasts who must love on command. We are domesticated animals.

If man had remained a beast, then the love in his heart would have been aroused once a year. But our sensuality, which we can restrain only with great effort, makes us capable of love at any time. Around the prime of life we are betrayed by it. And our sensuality is not simple but complicated, not natural but against nature.

This unnatural sensuality erupts in different ways in every century, indeed in every decade. It is in the air and it is infectious. Sometimes it spreads through a country like a pestilence that cannot be hidden; sometimes it sneaks through a nation like a secret and contagious disease, and those who are afflicted by it know how to conceal it from others. Sometimes the flagellants march along through the world and the burning funeral pyres turn into national celebrations; sometimes desire retreats into the most secret recesses of the soul. But however it may be, the Marquis de Sade, who represents the culmination point of the sensuality of his time, whose mind contrived the most grandiose martyrs of which our imaginations are capable, and the sweet, wan young maiden whose heart beats more freely once she has crushed a flea between her fingers—they are of one race.

That which is noble in a woman knows only one desire: that she hold on to her place by the side of the big, strong man. At present this desire can only be fulfilled if the woman wins the love of the man. This love makes her the man's subordinate. It is an unnatural love. If it were natural, the woman would be able to approach the man naked. But the naked woman is unattractive to the man. She may be able to arouse a man's love, but not to keep it.

People will have told you that it was the woman's modesty that made the fig leaf necessary. What an error! Modesty, this tiresome feeling developed by refined cultures, was unknown to the first men. Woman covered herself, she became a riddle to man, in order to implant in his heart the desire for the riddle's solution.

The awakening of love is at present the sole weapon that women possess in the battle of the sexes. But love is the daughter of lust. The woman's hope is to arouse the lust and desire of the man. The man can master the woman through the position that he has attained for himself in human society. He is animated by a drive for distinction, which he also expresses in his clothing. Every barber would like to look like a count. Once she is married, the woman acquires her social stamp through her husband, regardless of whether she has been a coquette or a princess. *Her* position is relinquished completely.

Thus the woman is forced to appeal to the man's sensuality through her clothing,

Ladies' Fashion

Neue Freie Presse, *August 21, 1898*
Republished in Dokumente der Frau, *March 1, 1902*

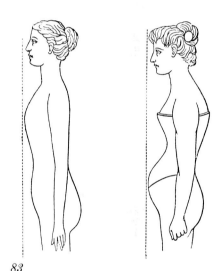

83
82 Cartoon by Bruno Paul from Simplicissimus, *1902, captioned "A conflict of fashion."*
83 At left, "normal uncorseted female figure"; at right, "corseted female figure." From Max von Boehn, Bekleidungskunst und Mode, *1918.*
84 Woman's undergarment designed by the American reformer Maria M. Jones, 1869. From Max von Boehn, Bekleidungskunst und Mode, *1918. (overleaf)*
85 Viennese fashion plate. From Wiener-Chic: Mode Journal, *Vienna, 1901. (overleaf)*

84

85

to appeal unconsciously to his sickly sensuality, for which only the culture of the times can be blamed.

On the one hand, then, change in men's fashion is effected in such a way that the masses go rushing headlong in their desire to be elegant; in this way the originally elegant style is debased in value, and those who are genuinely elegant—or better, those who are considered by the multitude to be elegant—must cast about for a new style in order to distinguish themselves. On the other hand, the vicissitudes of women's fashion are dictated only by changes in sensuality.

And sensuality changes constantly. Certain aberrations usually accumulate in one period, only then to make way for others. *The sentences meted out according to paragraphs 125 through 133 of our Penal Act are the most reliable fashion journal.*[1] I will not go very far back. At the end of the seventies and beginning of the eighties, the literature of a certain tendency, seeking to achieve its effect by means of its realism and directness, superabounded with descriptions of the beauty of voluptuous women and scenes of flagellation. Let me remind you only of Sacher-Masoch, Catulle Mendès, Armand Silvestre.[2] Soon thereafter, clothing sharply emphasized rounded voluptuousness and ripe femininity. Whoever did not already possess these had to counterfeit them: *le cul de Paris.* Then the reaction set in. The cry for youthfulness rang out. The child-woman came into fashion. People languished after immaturity. The psyche of the little girl was investigated and praised. Peter Altenberg.[3] The Barrisons danced on the stage and into men's hearts.[4] Whatever was womanly disappeared from women's clothing. Woman disguised away her hips; stout forms, earlier a source of pride to her, were now embarrassing. Her head took on a childlike look because of her hairstyle and her big sleeves. But these times too are over. It will be objected that just now the number of court cases involving crimes against children is increasing in the most frightful way. Certainly. This is the best proof that these crimes are disappearing from the upper classes and are now beginning their journey downward. For the masses do not have the means at their disposal to save themselves from this form of oppression.

A great and constant tendency has characterized the last hundred years, however. That which is still growing has persistently had a stronger appeal than that which is full grown. Spring has become the most favored season in this century. In earlier eras, the painters of flowers never painted buds. The professional beauties at the courts of the French kings once reached their fullest bloom at the age of forty. But today, even for those men who consider themselves completely normal, this point in the development of the woman has been pushed back about twenty years. Every woman thus chooses styles that bear all the signs of youth. One proof: place some photographs taken in the last twenty years next to each other in front of a woman. She will exclaim, "How old I looked twenty years ago!" And you too will have to admit that she looks youngest in the most recent picture.

As I have already remarked, there are also related tendencies. The most important, whose end is still by no means in sight, and, because it emanates from England, is thereby the strongest, is that persuasion invented by the refined Greeks: platonic love. The woman may be no more than a good friend to the man. This tendency too has been taken into account; it has led to the creation of the "tailor-made costume," clothes made by the man's tailor. But in that class of society in which the woman's aristocratic blood is also taken into consideration, in the high nobility where the woman's birth is a factor after many generations, one can dis-

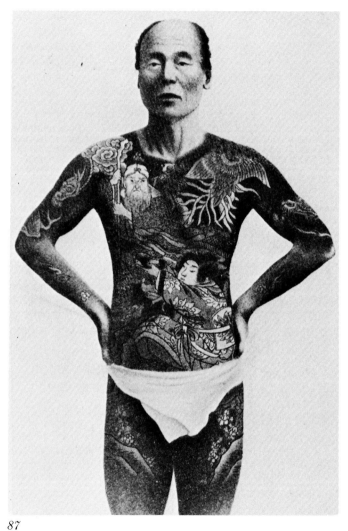

86   87

*86 Papuan native. From Max von
Boehn*, Bekleidungskunst und Mode,
1918.
*87 Tattooed Japanese man. From
Max von Boehn*, Bekleidungskunst
und Mode, *1918.*

cern an emancipation from the prevailing ladies' fashion in which homage is also paid to outward elegance. People thus never cease to wonder at the simplicity that prevails among the aristocracy.

It is implicit from what I have said that it is precisely *that* man that occupies the highest social position who commands the lead in men's fashion; but the leadership in women's fashion belongs to that woman who has to develop the most sensitivity to the awakening of sensuality: the coquette.

The clothing of the woman is distinguished externally from that of the man by the preference for ornamental and colorful effects and by the long skirt that covers the legs completely. These two factors demonstrate to us that the woman has fallen behind sharply in her development in recent centuries. No period of culture has known as great difference as our own between the clothing of the free man and that of the free woman. In earlier eras, men also wore clothing that was colorful and richly adorned and whose hem reached to the floor. Happily, the grandiose development in which our culture has taken part in this century has overcome ornament. I have to repeat myself here.* The lower the culture, the more apparent the ornament. Ornament is something that must be overcome. The Papuan and the criminal ornament their skin. The Indian covers his paddle and his boat with layers and layers of ornament. But the bicycle and the steam engine are free of ornament. The march of civilization systematically liberates object after object from ornamentation.

88 Woman in work clothes. From Max von Boehn, Bekleidungskunst und Mode, *1918.*

*See p. 40 of this book.

**In England the frock coat is worn at audiences with the queen, at the opening of Parliament, at weddings, and so forth, while in the backward nations tails are worn on the occasions mentioned as well as during the day.

Men who want to emphasize their relation to preceding eras still dress today in gold, velvet, and silk—grandees and clergy. Men from whom others want to withhold a recently acquired right, their self-determination, are also dressed in gold, velvet, and silk—lackeys and ministers. And the monarch, as the highest official of the state, wraps himself in ermine and crimson robes on special occasions, regardless of whether it suits his taste or not. The sense of servitude is also heightened among soldiers by means of uniforms that are colorful and stiff with gold.

The long robe that reaches to the ankles is the common mark of those who do not do physical labor. When physical activity and earning a living were incompatible with the enjoyment of a free and noble birth, the master wore a long garment and the servant wore pants. It is still this way in China today: mandarin and coolie. The clergyman of our time similarly emphasizes by means of his cassock that his activity is not oriented toward earning a livelihood. Certainly the man from the uppermost social class has won himself the right to earn his livelihood by working freely; yet for festive occasions he still wears an article of clothing that reaches down to his knees—the frock coat.**

The woman in these circles is not yet permitted to have any genuine employment. In those classes where she has acquired the right to earn a living, she too wears pants. Consider the female coal miner in the Belgian mines or the dairymaid in the Alps or the female shrimp-fisher of the North Sea.

Men too had to fight for the right to wear pants. Riding, an activity that contributes only to physical development but produces no material profit, was the first stage. Men have the thriving equestrian knighthood of the thirteenth century to thank for clothing that leaves the feet free. The sixteenth century, during which riding went out of fashion, could not again deprive them of this advance. But only in the last fifty years have women acquired the right to develop themselves

102

physically. It is an analogous process: as to the rider of the thirteenth century, the concession will be made to the twentieth-century female bicyclist to wear pants and clothing that leaves her feet free. And with this, the first step is taken toward the social sanctioning of women's work.

That which is noble in a woman knows only one desire: that she hold on to her place by the side of the big, strong man. At present this desire can only be fulfilled if the woman wins the love of the man. But we are approaching a new and greater time. No longer by an appeal to sensuality, but rather by economic independence earned through work will the woman bring about her equal status with the man. The woman's value or lack of value will no longer fall or rise according to the fluctuation of sensuality. Then velvet and silk, flowers and ribbons, feathers and paints will fail to have their effect. They will disappear.

Review of the Arts and Crafts

Die Wage, *October 1, 1898*

We have a new decorative art. It cannot be denied. Whoever has seen the rooms of Liberty's furniture store in London,[1] Bing's L'Art Nouveau on Rue de Provence in Paris,[2] last year's exhibition in Dresden, and this year's in Munich, will have to admit it: the old styles are dead, long live the new style!

And yet we cannot take pleasure in it. It is not our style. Our time did not give birth to it. We do possess objects that clearly display the stamp of our time. Our clothing, our gold and silver jewelry, our gems, our leather, tortoise shell, and mother-of-pearl goods, our carriages and railroad cars, our bicycles and locomotives all please us very well. Only we do not make so much of a fuss about them.

These things are modern; that is, they are in the style of the year 1898. But how do they relate to the objects that are currently being passed off as modern? With a heavy heart we must answer that these objects have nothing to do with our time. They are full of references to abstract things, full of symbols and memories. They are medieval.

But we are beyond this epoch. Since the decline of the Western Roman Empire there has been no era that has thought and felt more classically than ours. Think of Puvis de Chavannes and Max Klinger![3] Has anyone thought more Hellenistically since the days of Aeschylus? Look at the Thonet chair! Without decoration, embodying the sitting habits of a whole era, is it not born out of the same spirit as the Greek chair with its curved feet and its backrest? Look at the bicycle! Does the spirit of Pericles' Athens not waft through its forms? If the Greeks had wanted to build a bicycle, it would have been exactly the same as ours. And the Greek tripods of bronze—I am not talking about those given as Christmas presents, but rather those that were used—do they not look exactly like our iron products?

But it is not Greek to want to express one's individuality in the objects with which one surrounds oneself and which are meant for daily use. In Germany one sees the greatest variety of clothing; thus of all the civilized peoples, the Germans are the ones least filled with the Greek spirit. The Englishman, however, has only *one* outfit for a particular occasion, *one* bed, *one* bicycle. To him the best is the most beautiful. Thus, like the Greek, he chooses the best suit, the best bed, and the best bicycle. Modifications in form arise not from a desire for novelty, but rather from the wish to make the good more perfect yet. It is the business of our age to produce not a new chair, but the best chair.

However, in the exhibitions referred to, one saw only new chairs. The best chair will not be able to make any great claims to newness. For even ten years ago we had quite comfortable chairs, and the technique of sitting, the technique of relaxing, has not changed so very much since then that it could also already be expressed in a different form. The improvements will not be something the human eye will be able to recognize. They will be limited to millimeters or at most centimeters in the dimensions or the grade of the wood. How difficult it is to find a good chair! And how easy to find a new one! For newness there is a very simple formula: make a chair that is exactly the opposite of that which the people before you made.

In Munich an umbrella stand was displayed which can probably best demonstrate what I have said concerning the abundant references and the medieval aspect of utilitarian objects. If it had been the task of the Greek or the Englishman to fashion such a stand, the first thing he would have thought about was to pro-

89 Tapestry by Hermann Obrist. This illustration accompanied the original publication of Loos's article in Die Wage.

vide a good place for umbrellas to stand in. He would have reflected that the umbrellas ought to be able to be put in easily and taken out easily. He would have reflected that the umbrellas should not suffer any damage and that the covering material of the umbrella should not permit one to get stuck anywhere. But the non-Greek, the German, the average German, would do otherwise. For him, these considerations take a back seat. The main thing for him is to point out the relationship of this object to the rain by means of its decorative form. Water plants twine their way from bottom to top, and on each plant sits a frog. It does not trouble the German that the umbrellas can be ripped quite easily on the sharp leaves. He allows himself perfectly contentedly to be abused by his surroundings—as long as he finds them beautiful.

The level of culture that mankind attained in classical antiquity can no longer simply be eradicated from man's mind. Classical antiquity was and is the mother of all subsequent periods of culture. But there was cross-fertilization from the East. The East constituted the great reservoir out of which new seeds of development flowed into the West. It almost seems as if Asia has bequeathed to us today the last remains of her own primal strength. For we have already had to reach back to the furthermost points of the East, to Japan and Polynesia, and now we have come to an end. How good the Middle Ages had it! The Orient lay there still unexploited, and a walk to Spain or to the Holy Land was enough to open up new worlds of form for the West. Arab influences transformed the Romanesque style into the Gothic. The masters of the Renaissance had to reach out still further. They conquered Persia and India for us. Think of the Persian carpets without which no portrait of the madonna from this period is complete, and of the German intarsia and damascene work. The Rococo had to go as far as China; for us, only Japan still remains.

Now what is Japanese about our view of art? "That is a charming dress you are wearing, Madam. But what do I see? The one sleeve has a bow and the other one doesn't. It's very Japanese. You have a charming bouquet of flowers in your vase. Nothing but long-stemmed flowers: roses, lilies, chrysanthemums. That's Japanese too. If we had never directed our gaze toward Japan, we would find this kind of arrangement unbearable. Just ask the peasant girl on the Semmering.[4] She hasn't yet heard of Japan. And that's why she arranges her flowers in such an un-Japanese way. One great big one in the middle, and then the others always in a circle all around it. She finds it pretty."

In the first place, then, "Japanese" means giving up symmetry. Next, it means the dematerialization of the objects being represented. The Japanese represent flowers, but they are pressed flowers. They represent people, but they are pressed people. It is a kind of stylizing that is expressly meant to decorate the surface. But at the same time a naturalism is maintained. This is above all the technique of embroidery, and it has to come readily to anyone who delights in nature's forms. It is this technique of embroidery by which Hermann Obrist, the greatest of all artistic embroiderers of the present day, achieves his results.

The September issue of the leading arts and crafts paper *Art et Décoration* gives an account of a French artist. In it there is an article devoted to René Lalique.[5] Lalique, who owns one of the largest goldsmith firms in Paris, has the courage to strive to achieve his effects strictly through form and not through materials. He uses copper next to gold and works less with precious stones than with opals, agates, and carnelians. This is appealing. And yet he is wrong. In spite of the new form, the spirit of his objects is not derived from our own spirit; instead they

90 Lalique pendant. Loos reproduced this object, originally published in Art et Décoration, *Paris, June 1898, as an illustration for his article in* Die Wage.

105

gravitate toward the fifteenth and sixteenth centuries. They remind us of rustling silks and heavy velvets, rich furs and stiff brocades. It is the world of Charles V and Maximilian, the last knights, which suddenly appears before our eyes. But Lalique's jewelry looks quite strange in the age of the lightly fluttering silk dress, in the age of the starched shirtfront and black tails. Who would not like them? But who would want to wear them? The pleasure they excite is only platonic. Our age demands small jewelry—jewelry that represents the greatest possible value on the smallest possible area. Our age requires of jewelry that it have "distilled costliness," an "essence of the magnificent." For this reason the most valuable stones and materials will be used in our jewelry. The jewelry's meaning lies for us in the material. Thus, artistic work must content itself with bringing out the material's worth as much as possible. In jewelry that is to be worn, the work of the goldsmith takes only second place. Lalique's jewelry is real display-case jewelry, made as if to fill the treasury of a patron of the arts, who then graciously invites the public to admire the magnificent things in his museum.

People have become very sensitive in recent years in Vienna. If one gets hold of something from outside and tells them, "Look, this is how they do it in Tripstrill or Buxtehude," one must submit to being exposed publicly as treasonous and unpatriotic. It is the same whether it is paintings or chairs, operas or taxicabs. For the friends of Viennese industry assert, "By the introduction of foreign paintings, chairs, operas, and taxicabs, harm is done to our local painting, chair, opera, and taxicab industries."

I cannot understand this. If the things are of worse quality than ours—then hurrah! Then we can confidently puff out our chests and rejoice over this fact. Then, this fact having been established, Viennese industry will acquire new impetus. But if the foreign things are better? Then they will bring about an improvement of the local industry indirectly rather than directly. For the Viennese crafts industry will be able to take them as models, and we will be able to make up for the distance that separates the local from the foreign arts and crafts with one stroke.

Hofrat von Scala has put work from English schools on exhibit. Now, are they better or worse than ours? I think they are better. That is to say, our trade schools and arts and crafts schools are an imitation of the English institutions. But since we have been standing still while the English have been rapidly advancing, our schools find themselves at best at that point where the English were twenty years ago.

Thus we maintain that the English schoolwork is better than ours. We are, then, obliged to make up the distance. Of course, we have it relatively easy. The English lost time seeking paths, clearing terrain, and scouting an unknown course and an undiscovered territory. Now, without any dissipation of our energy, without experimentation, we can follow along on the comfortable, well-beaten paths.

Our schools have lost contact with life. The students have taken a dislike to the present. "Oh, how lovely it was in the Middle Ages! And especially in the Renaissance! Everywhere there was a rustling of brocades and crackling silks. Hooray, how the drums rolled and the naked women filed in procession to meet the king. And the jewels and colors and fluttering plumes! And now? Simply gruesome. Checkered suits, telephone wires, the jangling bells of the tramway. But what is that to us? We want to stand fast like rocks in the midst of the ugly bustle of modern life with our rustling silks and fluttering plumes. Down with the telephone! But if it must be? Then we want to arrive at a compromise. We will provide the telephone booths with Rococo ornament and the telephone receivers with Rococo handles. Or Gothic. Or Baroque. Any way the customer wishes it." And how did the slogan go that was coined in the last few years at the School of Applied Arts? "Old furniture for new needs."

The "stylish" telephone booth has so far been spared us. For this we have only to thank the fact that the telephone was invented in America, not in Germany or Austria. We were not so lucky with our motorized streetcars. Our gas candelabra, too, fall into this category and will make obvious even to the blind man the great step backward that has occurred in the transformation of our taste since the last exhibition of English candelabra.

It is contact with life that our schools have lost. Just ask our industrialists, artisans, and businessmen. Only one opinion prevails: the young people from our schools are useless. They are capable, it is true. But they are capable of doing

English Schools in the Austrian Museum

Die Wage, *January 29, 1898*

91 Tapestry by Walter Crane, titled "Kakadu." Exhibited at the Universal Exposition in Paris, 1900, and at the Austrian Museum for Art and Industry, Vienna, 1901. From Kunst und Kunsthandwerk, *no. 4, 1901.*

precisely those things that will pay the least. They are masters of the Munich beer hall style, the style of those people who can demand three courses and dessert for one mark. They can make *lusterweibchen* and the beloved, good old Old German ornamental divan, which day in and day out for a decade has been advertised at a "fraction of the original price" by twenty songsters in twenty Viennese "brief notices." These young people are told that the taste of the moneyed public, the taste cultivated, that is, by Förster or Würzl,[1] is "unartistic." But these businesses—I could, of course, name a dozen names—have always worked according to the "English" taste, or better, according to the elegant taste. For the Viennese now call everything that is elegant "English."

How might our schools regain contact with life? The current exhibition of the English offers the best answer. We see here how the best annual work of the various schools travels to London where it is put to the test. In this way one has all the schools at hand in a single place. From there it is easy to tell where good work is being done. And into *that* school which lags behind a little one can introduce new blood in the form of a capable teacher or a new director. We, of course, have something similar—our inspectors. But is the English system not simpler and more practical?

Thus the works that are sent in are examined, and the best of them are awarded prizes. By whom? Well, you say, probably by agents appointed for the purpose by the state. Wrong! The English do it differently. They say to themselves, a school inspector may well have very good taste; he will consider those things to be best which accord most with his own habits, his own needs. But the world does not consist of school inspectors. Artists and industrialists are much better qualified to do the same thing. They know what is of use to us, what we ought to avoid, and what we need. This year there were approximately thirty jurors ("examiners," as the report calls them). Names like Arthur Hacker,[2] Fred Brown,[3] and Walter Crane stand out. Not one of them is associated with the schools in any way. In committees of three, these examiners are responsible for passing an expert opinion on the work, which is divided into groups. Let us observe how they perform their task. We will take the architecture group. We read:
"Examiners: Professor G. Aitchison, R. A.; T. G. Jackson, R. A.; J. J. Stevenson.
"Architectural design.
"The quality of this year's work does not approach the high level of the work of the previous year.
"The examiners were glad to find many designs for workers' housing and would be pleased if more competitions were announced for exercises of this kind.
"Several of the plans show that the architects took too little time with them. It is the opinion of the examiners that planning should not be hurried.
"The examiners repeat, as they have indicated year after year, that whenever half-timber construction is used (for example, stone on the ground floor and wood above), it must be authentic. They repeat their request from last year that the excessively mannered lettering used in the plan descriptions be discontinued, as many of the legends could only be deciphered with difficulty.
"The examiners have noted that several plans were laid out symmetrically even though symmetry did not logically comport with the buildings.
"The points of the compass should be indicated on all plans."

Then follow short critiques of the individual drawings. For example: "The drawing by Allan Healey, Bradford Technical College, for a reading desk with baffled
108

lighting shows some invention, but the materials are not described. The details are crude."

Thus must everyone undergo a fairly sharp critique. Of the designs for linoleum plans it says, for example, "They are so poor that no grade can be given out."

It is an honor to be judged by and to receive prizes from such people. The manufacturers immediately purchase the prize-winning works, and many of the wallpapers whose original drawings were produced by the class of 1897 have already found their way into the world market and may already be purchased in Vienna too.

We thus see how in England the school exists in the midst of life. Art and life complement one another harmoniously. But with us the saying goes: art versus life!

92 Gentleman's bedroom by Rudolf Hammel. For the Winter Exhibition of the Austrian Museum for Art and Industry, Vienna, 1898. From Kunst und Kunsthandwerk, *no. 2, 1899.*

There was a school where geography was taught year in and year out. Europe, Asia, Africa, Australia, and America. But there was one gap in the schoolbook used in this school. England was missing. Why? Well, because the English did not enjoy the sympathies of the inhabitants of the city where the school was located. People thought they were playing a special trick on the English by ignoring them. Then there came a new head of the school. He was troubled to see that his students were perfectly at home in Tokyo and Venice, Samarkand and Paris, but did not even know the names Chippendale and Sheraton—pardon, I mean London and Liverpool. He decided to remedy this sorry state of affairs.

The far-seeing, hardworking students could not thank the new teacher enough for opening up a new world to them by including England in their curriculum. The lazy ones thought it superfluous. But since gratitude is always expressed quietly while ill will is associated with great clamor, everyone outside the school thought that all of the students were against the newly introduced subject. Besides, the hardworking students had their hands full with the new studies and no time for demonstrations.

The gentleman's bedroom found on the ground floor of the columned courtyard is a charming room. It has its flaws, certainly. The ceiling does not finish off the room. The green-stained wood cries out for a little piece of white wall; then the ceiling, since the walls too are covered with material, would have been exactly right for the space. Indeed, this was the secret of the outstanding success that Otto Wagner had at the Jubilee Exhibition. For even though the ceiling is of the same green color as the furniture, no one can stay for long in that green sauce. Moreover, the most unfortunate motif imaginable was chosen for the ceiling: an iron grating around which foliage tendrils wind themselves. In a rainstorm one will only weather it out under such a ceiling if he opens an umbrella.

These are objections that have nothing to do, of course, with the actual room and its carpentry work. The magnificent wood carvings from the hand of Zelezny, the authentic carpenter's profiling, give the room something old-masterly in spite of the new forms. The architect Hammel designed the room. He put himself into the mind of the carpenter and endeavored to overcome the architect in himself. But since the room has his signature all over it, the result is that the brass fixtures cannot match the carpentry work in value. That is, they too are carpenter-like and even display the same ornament as the wood. The bed can be concealed from the visitor's eyes by portieres during the day. I consider this superfluous. It would be frightful if the notion would creep back in again—it was current during the first half of our century—that sleeping and going to bed were something to be hidden modestly from one's fellow men. On the other hand, the washstand is all the more practical since the side against the wall is covered with tiles.

*

There is a chair on the second floor of the columned courtyard. This chair constitutes one of those points of indictment raised by the opposing side against Hofrat von Scala. Let us listen to the words of one of the "leading experts." He writes, "It is difficult to believe the inferior objects that one now sees being exhibited under the new museum director! Chairs with straw seats of the most simple execution can now be seen on exhibit, quite good work, but by no means works of art."

This is a serious reproach. But did Hofrat von Scala immediately remove the aforementioned chair—for it is for once no invention—in order not to provoke further the wrath of the leading technical authority? Not at all! It continues to be on exhibit and continues to offend the aesthetic sensibility of those gentlemen who are able to sit on nothing but works of art.

It would be pointless to talk with that expert about the fact that even the simplest straw chair made by the hand of a human being ranks a thousand times higher than the one that is made with the most sumptuous stamped leather and produced by the machine. He wouldn't understand me. But maybe one can reach him in another way. That chair costs twenty gulden, even though—I admit this freely—it displays the simplest form and only has a straw seat; it costs this thanks to its exemplary design. But I know of polished and carved chairs with lavish leather seats that are being sold for around ten gulden. And so I maintain that this simple chair is of more use to the Austrian arts and crafts than the lavish ten-gulden chair. For it tells us that good work is something for which we must pay; it increases the public's sense of value. And that is a worthy mission! Don't you agree?

*

Isn't it remarkable that the most audacious innovators, that is, the most capable people, are also those who profess the deepest respect for the work of their predecessors? Actually not. For competence can only be valued again by competence. The public will recall the sensation that was created at the Secession Exhibition by the ultramodern furniture of one Viennese atelier. And the very same atelier this time brings us an exact copy of a room from the Esterhazy palace near Ödenburg. This is unremarkable for another reason as well. Namely, to copy something exactly is exceedingly more difficult than to copy something approximately. Every painter knows this. Since mediocrity is always in the majority, there is a significantly greater number of voices that speak out for approximate copying than for correct copying. But the public may of course decide for itself.

I cannot remember ever having seen the aristocratic milieu of noble feudal estates from the past century better captured than in this room. Were it not for the smell of glue, one would swear that one was in an old manor house belonging to the nobility. What joy of work, what refinement, what sensibility it presupposes! The atelier was kept busy for seven years by the renovation of the palace and, as the fruit of this long labor, has made us a gift of this room. In terms of quantity it is not much, but it has quality. Only narrow-mindedness can count it a mistake that genuinely old pieces of furniture, masterpieces of the art of carpentry from the last century, have also been exhibited in the room. On the contrary: they prove to us that modern Viennese work can stand successfully next to the old masters.

*

Across from the straw chair that is so threatening to the arts and crafts is a wall sconce for three candles. Even though it is made out of brass, it cannot deny its wrought-iron derivation. No one can think any better in wrought iron. The blacksmith took so and so many inches of hoop iron, split it at both ends, and spread the ends apart; on one side he welded a new piece the width of the split iron to obtain the third arm. He widened the other two ends on the anvil in order

112

to be able to put in bore holes for the nails, which then would serve to fasten it to the wall. He filed these widened ends the right amount and bent the thus prepared hoop iron into the proper form. Ready! And afterward we are impressed with the thing even though it is not possible to think any more simply or primitively. It is a breath of naturalness that emanates from this sconce. We are glad finally to hear the blacksmith speak in his own language after he has spoken to us for decades in bombastic, undigested clichés. But we would ask one thing: that the smith be given back conceptions that are inherently his, and that the sconces be produced in wrought iron.

The Scala Theater in Vienna[1]

Die Wage, *November 5, 1898*

93 Title page from the first issue of
Kunst und Kunsthandwerk *under the
direction of Anton von Scala, 1898.*

Prelude
Time: pre-Scala period
Vestibule of the Austrian Museum
Visitor, Office Worker
Visitor: May I speak with the director?
Worker: No, the Director does not arrive until around twelve.
Visitor: And when does he leave?
Worker: Also . . . around twelve.

Meeting of the Arts and Crafts Association
Speaker: . . . and so I believe that I have examined all of the reasons that can be cited against the annual holding of a Christmas Exhibition. The developments in the arts and crafts are not significant enough to sustain the interest of the public every year. I therefore propose this exhibition only be held every three years.
(The proposal is accepted.)

On the street
First Carpenter: Where are you coming from?
Second Carpenter: From the Christmas Exhibition.
First Carpenter: Did you actually exhibit something?
Second Carpenter: Exhibit! Who? Me? Am I an imperial councillor? Am I a commercial councillor? Am I a knight of the Order of Franz Joseph? You know all too well that such things are not for people like us. It is true, in order to be able to exhibit you need only be a member of the Arts and Crafts Association, but are we supposed to get involved in that? You know how we common people are treated over there.
First Carpenter: But perhaps one can exhibit without belonging to the association.
Second Carpenter: You would meet with a fine reception with that idea! In this museum the state, that is to say the taxpayer, has nothing to say. The Arts and Crafts Association does everything. The institution is supported by the state but whoever doesn't belong to the clique has no business there.
First Carpenter: And so the whole thing is the clubhouse for a private club?
Second Carpenter: Yes, yes, it's beginning to look that way.

Act I
Time: Scala period
Scene 1
In the Ministry of Culture and Education
. . . and so I request, my dear Hofrat, that you direct your special attention to the remedying of the grievances that have crept into the institution now entrusted to your care. We know that you are a man with initiative. May you succeed in emancipating our arts and crafts from the present state of stagnation, offering new stimuli, and establishing a connection with the modern movements in the arts and crafts.

Scene 2
In the office of the new director
First Museum Official: Herr Hofrat, the room assigned to me is hardly sufficient to accommodate a quarter of our ceramics collection.
Hofrat: Then use Room A as well.
First Museum Official: It is occupied by the Arts and Crafts Association.
Hofrat: Well, then . . .
(First Museum Official exit)

114

Second Museum Official: Herr Hofrat, there is no place in the arcaded court for the collection of furniture from the last century.
Hofrat: Then use Room B as well.
Second Museum Official: It is occupied by the Arts and Crafts Association.
Hofrat: Well, then . . .
(Second Museum Official exit)
Third Museum Official: Herr Hofrat, I have just discovered that a major and valuable part of our textile collection has fallen victim to rot in the damp storehouses.* Precious lace embroidery, cloth from royal Egyptian tombs, everything, everything is lost beyond salvation!
Hofrat: Whatever can still be saved is to be put in Room C immediately.
Third Museum Official: It is occupied by the Arts and Crafts Association.
Hofrat: Well, then . . .
(Third Museum Official exit)
This scene can be extended at will.

*Because of the shortage of space, the Austrian Museum had to keep a major portion of its collections in storage houses.

Scene 3
Hofrat (writing): . . . and so, in the face of the severe shortage of space, I consider it my duty as director of this institution entrusted to me by the state to request that the Arts and Crafts Association place at my disposal as quickly as possible the rooms which it has heretofore occupied. I consider the museum's further relinquishing of such important rooms to a wholly private organization to be an abridgement of the rights of the rest of the arts and crafts workers and the public. I am of the opinion that all citizens of Austria, without regard to organizational membership, have the same right to this institution .

Scene 4
In the Arts and Crafts Association
First Member: That is unheard of!
Second Member: Infamous!
Third Member: Scandalous!
Fourth Member: And so we're supposed to move out?
First Member: Indeed, are we the masters of the house, or aren't we? Our position will have to be made perfectly clear to him!
Second Member: He wants to allow other people to exhibit here!
Third Member: And the others are also to be allowed to sell their work!
All (shouting): Merchants!

Scene 5
In the Director's chamber
Hofrat: What a pity! I thought all the available rooms would be at my disposal for the museum's Christmas Exhibition. And now the Arts and Crafts Association wants to organize one, too. Hadn't they decided to hold an exhibition only every three years? So I was not expecting this. It seems I will have to reduce the size of my show. I very much hope to have next year's Christmas Exhibition all to myself to make up for this. Christmas Exhibition? No, that name was created by the Association itself. It wouldn't be fair for me to usurp it. I must figure out another one. Let's say "Winter Exhibition."
(A knock at the door. The Office Worker announces the carpenter Kleinhuber.)
Carpenter Kleinhuber (with much bowing and scraping and speaking high Viennese dialect): Herr Hofrat, you will please excuse me, Your Honor, if I permit myself, please excuse me very much, I know I am only a common craftsman, but a certain Kratochwil, whom Herr Hofrat, pardon me, already knows, said to me, "Kleinhuber," he said (that is my name, you see, Kleinhuber), Herr Hofrat

please excuse me . . .

Hofrat (interrupting him): But what would you like, my dear fellow? Perhaps you would like me to exhibit your work here?

Kleinhuber (pleased and excited): Yes, to exhibit!

Hofrat: Well then, that can be arranged.

Kleinhuber (once again timid): Yes, but Herr Hofrat, I am only a common craftsman, I work with only one assistant and two boys, you will pardon me.

Hofrat: That makes no difference to me. The museum is here for *all* tradesmen. The privileges that previously have been granted only to a private association shall from now on be accorded to all. If this association is permitted to hold an exhibition here, then the others shall do so as well. If this association is permitted to sell its products here, then the others may do so as well. Everyone has the same rights in a state institution. An institution supported by all the citizens of the state is also there for the benefit of all the citizens of the state. The association may find it very unpleasant, but the other craftsmen must be taken into consideration. Tell this to your colleagues and send as many as possible of them over here to me. All you people are intimidated. But I will continue to work until this institution becomes in reality what its founders intended: *a center for Austrian arts and crafts* which offers everyone—*everyone*—strength, stimulation, and instruction. People reproach *me* for being a merchant. I certainly did not introduce the right to sell goods here. I was obliged to extend it to include everyone. Justice demanded that. Now, what do you want to exhibit?

Kleinhuber (listening with growing astonishment): Oh, Herr Hofrat, if you would be so kind, I would like to exhibit a simple chest which has been sitting in my shop for twenty years and which no one wants to buy. I will certainly sell it here.

Hofrat: No, my dear man, that is not how it works. You are mistaken. But I cannot blame you for it. After all, up until now the purpose of the Christmas Exhibitions was to clear out the abundant stocks in some of the furniture storehouses. But now things are different. If goods must be sold, it is only as a means to an end. And the end is to make the public acquainted with the newest advances in the arts and crafts. Which does not mean that the old should be given short shrift. Those areas should be especially fostered which for one reason or another are still foreign to the public. For example, the Viennese know nothing of the whole English furniture industry of the last century. The first Winter Exhibition will therefore pursue the goal of presenting this period to the public through good copies. I can give you an English original to take along and use as a model; it belongs to the museum and naturally is not for sale. But you may also make something on your own. And then you must permit me to decide whether or not the object is worthy of exhibition. For I alone am answerable to the state for what may and may not be exhibited in this institution, this house of the state. The state expects me to bring about a transformation in this institution, which over the last decade has become a marketplace for the Arts and Crafts Association. I was appointed to this position on the basis of my activity in the Commerce Museum. If I were now to be led astray by different principles, if I were to yield to them, it would be a betrayal of the state. So then, do you want to make copies or do you want to create something new?

Kleinhuber: I would rather copy, Herr Hofrat, if I might. I don't feel confident making my own things yet. Perhaps I can do so later when I know what's involved.

Hofrat: In that case, come back soon, and by next time I will have something picked out for you.

Kleinhuber (to himself as he leaves, shaking his head): Incredible! . . . Did you ever see the like! And that's supposed to be a hofrat! That ain't no hofrat! That ain't even a real official.

Act II
Scene 1
After the close of the Winter Exhibition of 1897
At the meeting of the Arts and Crafts Association
First Member: A miserable business.
Second Member: People poured in as if they were being given gifts inside.
Third Member: Yes, this is how the arts and crafts lose their respect.
Fourth Member: And the things were bought up like hotcakes.
First Member: That never happened with us!
All (with conviction): No, never!
Second Member: If blessed Eitelberger had lived to see this!
Third Member: What has become of art?
Fourth Member: Unabashed utilitarian objects!
First Member: To ruin our business in this way!
Second Member: You said it, ruin!
First Member: To think that now I have a whole storeroom of Old German furniture and no one wants to buy it anymore.
Third Member: It's exactly the same with me.
First Member: I advised him that to sell my stock of goods better—pardon, to promote the growth of the domestic arts and crafts—he should push the Old German trend harder. But do you think he took that course?
Fourth Member: Such insolence!
Second Member: And to show English furniture! Of course, for years I have been importing furniture from London, but . . .
Third Member: Me too.
Fourth Member: Me too.
First Member: Me too.
Second Member: . . . that doesn't matter. *Quod licet bovi, non licet Jovi.*[2]
Third Member: And now every carpenter can imitate English furniture, while we used to have to go to great lengths to import these things from Maple and Henry![3]
Fourth Member: Yes, this is damaging to the Viennese arts and crafts.
First Member: Where are the good times, when *we* conducted the business in the museum!
Second Member: He takes it upon himself to do it all on his own!
Third Member: He sits there from eight in the morning until seven at night. When did you ever see a hofrat do that! It's businessman's behavior!
Fourth Member: And he fraternizes with all the common people. All the people who used to do work for me are now exhibiting their own work.
First Member: But next time we will show him that we too can attract visitors and buyers!
Second Member: But how?
Third Member: Maybe it's a question of the name. In the future we too should call our exhibition the "Winter Exhibition."
Fourth Member: Exactly. That's it! But soon. As soon as next year. The changes in the arts and crafts are so significant that it is absolutely necessary to hold a Christmas—pardon—Winter Exhibition every year.
First Member: And we must get rid of the hofrat!
Second Member: Out with him!
Third Member: Out with him!
Fourth Member: O-U-T!
First Member: But how?

Second Member: Yes, how?

Third Member: I have an idea! We simply spread the rumor that the exhibitors are his personal protégés!

Fourth Member: Or that the objects are actually manufactured in his secret factory in the museum.

First Member: Or that the things weren't made here at all but were all imported from England.

Second Member: Or that he is a sales agent for a London furniture dealer.

Third Member: A commercial traveler!

Fourth Member: But will anyone believe us?

First Member: Well, I could marshal the requisite "authorities" in a few newspapers.

Second Member: And in the end, if nothing else works, we do still have our patron!

Third Member: Right, we must go to our patron!

Fourth Member: Certainly, he will help us get back in charge!

Scene 2
In a cafe

First Manufacturer: What's that I've heard? You, a member of the Arts and Crafts Association, exhibiting with Scala?

Second Manufacturer: Sure, and why not? I pay my membership dues, and that's the end of it. I don't want to have anything at all to do with the Association. I don't even come to the exhibitions.

First Manufacturer: But doesn't your membership damage your relationship with the hofrat?

Second Manufacturer: Not in the least. Indeed, fifty percent of the exhibitors are members of the Arts and Crafts Association.

Scene 3
In the office of the Austrian Museum

First Member (as a spokesman for a deputation from the Arts and Crafts Association): Herr Hofrat, we would like to petition you to repeal your decree stipulating that exhibition objects may not be brought into the building during visiting hours.

Hofrat: That cannot be done. If *my* exhibitors must respect the visiting hours, then I cannot grant *you* any special privileges. References to earlier directorships have no influence on me.

Member: But then the entire exhibition is placed in jeopardy for us. The carriages first have to make a stop on the Prater and cannot arrive at the museum any earlier than nine o'clock.

Hofrat: The Prater? Are your workshops located on the Prater?

Member: Not the workshops, the Exhibition.

Hofrat (who is beginning to catch on): What? . . .You want—

Member: Of course! We want to try to sell the things in the Austrian Museum which we did not dispose of at the Jubilee Exhibition.

Hofrat: —?—!!!

(The conversation becomes very heated.)

Scene 4
At the meeting of the Arts and Crafts Association

First Member: Do you know what has happened?

All: No!

First Member: Thrown out!!

118

All (delighted): Finally!!

First Member: You don't understand, gentlemen. It is *we* that he has . . .

All (angrily): Unheard of!

First Member: Yes, he claims that he does not have to tolerate rudeness in his office!

A Member: Well, who on earth does he think he is? *Is he not supported by our taxes?* After all, he is only a civil servant! What is he there for, after all?!

All: He won't tolerate rudeness? We will go to the steps of the throne and lodge a complaint about this man!

Act III

This act is being played out in the present. We will in due course inform the readers of the outcome of this Viennese drama. Should the necessity arise to present further scenes from the earlier acts, they will be given all due attention.

My Appearance on Stage with Melba[1]

Neues Wiener Tagblatt,
*April 20, 1920**

*Erratum. The date of the essay "My
Appearance on Stage with Melba" should
correctly read April 20, 1900 (not 1920).
1931. [The article actually appeared on
January 20, 1900.—Ed.]

In the year 1895, when I was an outside reporter for the *New-Yorker banner-träger*,[2] I found the following note one day in my mailbox:
My dear Sir!
Please come to see me tomorrow morning between eleven and twelve at the editor's office.
John Smith
Editor-in-Chief, *New-Yorker bannerträger*

At the appointed time I found my way to the editor's office where the editor-in-chief laid the following question before me:
"Tell me, Mr. L., can you write music reviews?" At first, I wanted to tell him that I have absolutely no ear for music and that I have to gather up all my strength to distinguish a treble clef from a house key. Only I stifled this reply. It occurred to me that I had heard the following golden rule from a wise man upon my arrival in the New World: "If anyone in America asks you if you can do this or that, then respond immediately with a proud and delighted 'yes'! Then you cannot go wrong."

Therefore I said, "But naturally, Mr. Smith, that is precisely my field!"

"That works out perfectly. As you know, Mr. Schulze, the proprietor of the renowned piano school, writes our music reviews. But since we do not receive free tickets for the opera, Mr. Alexander Neumann has up till now taken on the opera reviews because he is acquainted with almost all of the box owners. However, Mr. Neumann is leaving us and going over to the English press. Would you like to take charge of the opera? Of course, we can only buy you an orchestra standing-room ticket for the performance. Have our cashiers give you a dollar and fifty cents. The opening of the season is tomorrow. We expect your report at the latest by one a.m."

I left. The cashier paid me the dollar and fifty cents. I was somewhat worried. The affair seemed slightly disturbing. I went straightaway to the Cafe Manhattan and pored over the music notices in all the newspapers. I soon realized that the most important thing was the technical terminology. That was what was impressive. E-flat major, a thrice-bowed C, counterpoint, dynamics, crescendo. After three hours I knew enough. I calmly looked forward to the following day.

An acquaintance at the next table stood up, paid, and put on his coat. We exchanged greetings. "How are you? Where are you going?" "To the Metropolitan Opera." "What's there?" "I am a duly hired walk-on at that cultural institution. Yes, what can you do? In America, one must take every opportunity that presents itself."

That excuse probably followed because I had made a strange face. But my strange face was provoked by a quite different thought. What would it be like, I calculated, if I joined up with this man? I could then save a dollar and a half and still attend the performance. And what's more: be allowed on stage as an extra! Who wouldn't want to do that?!

Hence I responded, "You are mistaken, dear friend; on the contrary, I find your occupation enviable. You seem not to know that for ten years I belonged to the company of mute extras at the Vienna Court Opera. That is precisely my field! Couldn't you take me along?"

My friend smiled patronizingly. "Come along, I'll try it." We climbed into the trolley car and arrived ten minutes later at the corner of 49th Street and Broadway. Here I was introduced to the director of the extras.

"Were you in the military?" he asked.

"Certainly," I said, "I was an officer for ten years. That is precisely my field!"

"Then you are hired." At which point he shouted backstage, "The guard is complete."

Soon his strange words became clear to me. *Carmen* was being performed and the guard which is led on by Don José in the first act was to consist strictly of veteran soldiers. Great stress was laid on the correct "click" of the heals. We soon established to everyone's satisfaction that among the fourteen men of the guard eleven were former officers, part from the German, part from the Austrian army. We were thoroughly drilled and within a short time the procession of the guard clicked perfectly.

The evening came. Jean de Reszke sang José, his brother Edouard sang Escamillo, Calvé sang Carmen, and Melba sang Micaela. Permit me to leave out the details. The most important event was that at the conclusion of the performance Jean de Reszke had us paid ten dollars.

The performance was over. I feverishly hurried to change my clothes, picked up my pay—fifty cents—and took the elevated subway to the editor's office. Just before one in the morning I had my manuscript finished, and with great satisfaction read the following (I paraphrase): "We greatly enjoyed Mrs. Melba's performance; her upper organ stops are particularly beautiful, but the counterbass, the counterbass! And her range seems to extend over spanned octaves. All in all, the sonorous middle register with the thrice-bowed C forms an effective cadenza."

Yes indeed, it was an achievement. The numerous technical terms were bound to make an impression, for better or for worse.

I went home a proud man and fell asleep carefree and happy. The next morning—the delivery boy had placed the *New-Yorker bannerträger* as usual before the door—I read out my masterpiece in a loud voice to my roommate, Baron N., who at first was still asleep.

The Baron noticeably began to wake up. Then he said, "I don't know what's wrong with me. But I am hearing some very strange things. Perhaps I didn't sleep too well. Read me the story again."

I reread it. The baron's face slowly took on an expression of horror. Then he burst out:
"Oh, you thrice-bowed unfortunate worm! What on earth have you done!" In short, he abused me and called me a cretin.

And then he explained my article to me, sentence by sentence. Slowly the realization dawned on me that I had made a fool of myself. I was crushed. I no longer dared go out on the street. Everyone would be able to read the humiliation on my face. And then—I grew pale at the thought—the editor.

The Baron had long since left for his office. Still numb, I brooded alone in my room. In the meantime eleven o'clock had come around. The newsboy brought the evening edition of the *New-Yorker staatszeitung*. Our evening edition does not appear until eleven-thirty in the morning. The English evening papers usually appear before sunrise.

I mechanically reached for the newspaper. There—what was that?! I read feverishly:
"Brusque Rebuff!
The Music Bungler of the *Morgenposaune* Taken to Task!!!
An Accomplishment by the *New-Yorker Bannerträger!!!*

That was only the "head," as they say in American journalese. I read on:
"We have repeatedly pointed out the shameful carryings on of that young fellow who sets out his total ignorance of things musical in his reviews in the *morgenposaune* to the detriment of the entire German community on the island of Manhattan. This miserable scribbler is a blemish on the untarnished reputation of German America. Up until now, we have stood alone in our crusade against this individual. Today we can state with satisfaction that the *New-Yorker bannerträger* has taken up the cross (even though its owner belongs to the Hebrew confession). Our trusty colleague at this brave paper admirably imitated in his opera review of today the bad ways and manners of that individual. To the universal joy of all true friends of music, he publicly exposed him and thereby delivered him up to the general mockery. We believe that the *morgenposaune* will never be able to recover from this blow. We cannot resist the temptation of reprinting this opera review, a satiric masterpiece, for our readers."

My article followed.

First I danced an impromptu bacchanale. Then I threw on my winter coat, dashed to the elevated subway, and nearly knocked down the editor's door with my paper. I stormed around with the *staatszeitung* in hand. John Smith, the editor-in chief, looked at me in astonishment. "What, you still dare to enter our offices?" he railed at me. I immediately comprehended the situation. The man had obviously not yet read the evening edition of the *New-Yorker staatszeitung*. So I smiled with a superior air and said, "I didn't think that we were obliged to show any deference to the *morgenposaune!*"

"What do we care about that rag for! You have made *us* look ridiculous!"

"What? Are you really the only one who has not understood the profound satire? You don't seem to be aware that satire is precisely my field. Well, at least the *staatszeitung* understood the matter more quickly."

He read the article. My readers will permit me to spare them a description of how very ashamed the man was.

On the next morning I read in the *morgenposaune*, "Our music critic has resigned his post."

The morning after that I received a thick letter. I opened it with anticipation. It contained the news that the New York Music Critics Association had named me an honorary member.

And so with this my first and last music review, I acquired some practical experience that a philosopher, literary historian, or art historian could never have matched. For them, the technical terminology always turns out fine whenever they write about painting, architecture, or crafts. No one will check up on the art critic as to whether a "strut" is not perhaps a "truss." "Suitability of materials," "carpentered," "mortice and tenon joint," "beveled edge," and similar shoptalk he can consider sprinkling throughout his reviews totally at will. He can calmly claim that Ruskin has already died—even if, by good fortune, he celebrates Ruskin's eightieth birthday the very next week with the universal participation of the civilized world. And without fear he can continue to say of the artist that the effect of his light is particularly successful: the moon shines magically through the open window into the room—even though the supposed window is a mirror, and the moon is reflected candlelight. These are things that can always appear in an American newspaper. And in music, should it really be necessary for the writer to be able to read notes and understand what basso continuo and counterpoint are?

It is an injustice in any event, even though the affair turned out well for me.

*94 Study designed by Josef Hoffmann
for one of the Secession exhibitions.
From* Kunst und Kunsthandwerk,
no. 2, 1899.

I want to tell you a story about a poor little rich man. He had money and possessions, a faithful wife who kissed his business cares from his brow, and a brood of children that any of his workers might envy. His friends loved him because whatever he touched prospered. But today things are quite, quite different. It happened like this.

One day this man said to himself, "You have money and possessions, a faithful wife and children that any of your workers might envy. But are you happy? Look, there are men who lack all these things for which you are envied. But their cares are charmed away by a great sorceress—Art. And what does Art mean to *you?* You know nothing more than her name. Any swell can present his visiting card at your home, and your servant flings open the doors. But you have not yet received Art into your home. I am sure that she will not come of her own accord. But I will seek her out. She shall enter my home like a queen and live with me."

He was an energetic man; whatever he seized upon was carried out with vigor. People were accustomed to that from him because of the way he ran his business. And so on the very same day he went to a famous architect and said, "Bring Art to me, bring Art into my home. Cost is no object."

The architect did not wait for him to say it twice. He went into the rich man's home, threw out all his furniture, called in an army of parquet-floor layers, espalier specialists, lacquerers, masons, painters, carpenters, plumbers, potters, carpet layers, artists, and sculptors, and presto, quicker than you could blink an eye, Art was captured, boxed in, and taken into good custody within the four walls of the rich man's home.

The rich man was overjoyed. Overjoyed, he walked through his new rooms. Wherever he cast his glance was Art, Art in each and every thing. He grasped Art when he took hold of a door handle; he sat on Art when he settled into an armchair; he buried his head in Art when, tired, he lay it down on a pillow; he sank his feet into Art when he trod on the carpet. He reveled in Art with an enormous fervor. After his plate was artistically decorated, he cut into his *boeuf à l'oignon* with twice as much vigor.

He was praised, he was envied. The art journals extolled him as one of the leading patrons of the arts; his rooms were reproduced as models, commented upon, and explained.

And they deserved it, too. Each room formed a symphony of colors, complete in itself. Walls, wall coverings, furniture, and materials were made to harmonize in the most artful ways. Each household item had its own specific place and was integrated with the others in the most wonderful combinations.

The architect had forgotten nothing, absolutely nothing. Cigar ashtrays, cutlery, light switches—everything, everything was made by him. But these were no ordinary architect's arts; no, the individuality of the owner was expressed in every ornament, every form, every nail. (It was a psychological piece of work whose difficulty will be evident to anybody.)

Yet the architect modestly disclaimed all honors. "No," he said, "these rooms are not mine at all. Over there in the corner is a statue by Charpentier. And just as I would take it amiss if anyone tried to pass off a room as his own design if he as much as used one of my door latches, I cannot now make so bold for myself and

125

claim that these rooms are my spiritual property." It was spoken nobly and logically. Upon hearing these words, many a carpenter who had furnished one of his rooms with a tapestry by Walter Crane but had intended to take credit for its furniture anyway since he had designed and executed it was shamed to the very depths of his black soul.

Let us return after this digression to our rich man. I have already said how happy he was. From this point on he devoted a large portion of his time to the study of his home. For it had to be learned; this he soon realized. There was a great deal to take note of. Each furnishing had a definite place. The architect had meant well by him. He had thought of everything. Even for the smallest little box there was a specially prepared place.

The home was comfortable, but it taxed the owner's brain. Therefore the architect supervised the inhabitants in the first weeks so that no mistake might creep in. The rich man gave his best efforts. But it happened that he would lay a book down and, deep in thought, push it into a compartment made for newspapers. Or that he would flick the ashes of his cigar into the indentation in the table intended to hold the candlesticks. Once someone had picked up an object in his hand, there was no end to the guessing and searching for its correct place, and several times the architect had to unroll his working drawings in order to rediscover the place for a matchbox.

Where applied art celebrated such triumphs, applied music could not be permitted to lag behind. This idea very much preoccupied the rich man. He submitted a petition to the streetcar company in which he sought to have the nonsensical ringing replaced with the bell motif from *Parsifal*. However, he found the company uncooperative. They were clearly not receptive enough to modern ideas there. Instead he was permitted, at his own expense, to have the street in front of his house repaved so that every vehicle was forced to roll by in the rhythm of the *Radetzky March*.[1] The electric chimes in his rooms also acquired Beethoven and Wagner motifs, and all the celebrated art critics were full of praise for the man who had opened up a new field with his "art in the utilitarian object."

One can imagine that all of these improvements made the man still happier.

However, it must not be kept a secret that he preferred to be home as little as possible. After all, one also wants to take a rest now and then from so much art. Or could you live in a picture gallery? Or sit through *Tristan and Isolde* for months on end? Well then! Who would blame him for gathering new strength in a cafe, in a restaurant, or among friends and acquaintances? He had thought things would be different. But art requires sacrifice. Yet he had already sacrificed so much. His eyes became moist. He thought of many old things which he had loved and which he sometimes missed. The big easy chair! His father always used to take his afternoon nap on it. The old clock! And the pictures! But: Art requires it! One must only keep from weakening!

Once it happened that he celebrated his birthday. His wife and children had lavished gifts upon him. The things pleased him exceedingly and were a source of true joy to him. The architect arrived soon thereafter to look after the correctness of things and to make decisions on difficult matters. He entered the room. The master of the house greeted him happily, for he had many things on his mind. But the architect did not notice the other's pleasure. He had discovered something quite different, and he turned pale. "What kind of slippers are you

126

wearing?" he blurted out with effort.

The master of the house looked at his embroidered shoes. But he breathed a sigh of relief. This time he felt totally innocent. For the shoes had been made to the architect's original design. So he answered with a superior air, "But Herr Architect! Have you already forgotten? You yourself designed the shoes!"

"Of course," thundered the architect, "but for the bedroom. Here they disrupt the whole mood with their two impossible spots of color. Don't you see that?"

The master of the house did see it. He quickly pulled off the shoes and was pleased to death that the architect did not find his socks impossible too. They went into the bedroom, where the rich man was again permitted to put on his shoes.

"Yesterday," he began here irresolutely, "I celebrated my birthday. My family literally showered me with gifts. I have called you, my dear architect, so that you can give us some advice as to how we can best display these things."

The architect's face grew noticeably longer. Then he exploded, "How do you come to allow yourself to be given gifts! Did I not design *everything* for you? Did I not consider *everything*? You don't need anything more. You are complete!"

"But," the master of the house permitted himself to respond, "I am allowed to buy something for myself, after all!"

"No, you are *not* allowed! Never ever! That's all I need! Things that have not been designed by me? Didn't I go far enough by permitting you the Charpentier? The statue that robs me of total glory for my work! No, you must buy nothing else!"

"But what if my grandchild gives me something he has made at kindergarten?"

"Then you must not accept it!"

The master of the house was crushed. But he did not yet give up. An idea, yes, an idea!

"And what if I wanted to buy myself a painting at the Secession?" he asked triumphantly.

"Then just try to hang it somewhere. Don't you see that there is room for nothing more? Don't you see that for every picture that I have hung for you here I have also designed a frame on the partition or the wall? You can't even *move* a picture. Just try to find a place for a new picture!"

Then a transformation took place in the rich man. The happy man suddenly felt deeply, deeply unhappy. He imagined his future life. No one was allowed to give him pleasure. He would have to pass by the shops of the city impervious to all desires. Nothing more would be made for him. None of his dear ones was permitted to give him a picture. For him there were to be no more painters, no more artists, no more craftsmen. He was precluded from all future living and striving, developing and desiring. He thought, this is what it means to learn to go about life with one's own corpse. Yes indeed. He is finished. *He is complete!*

Appendix

Foreword to the First Edition

KURT WOLFF, Publishers
LEIPZIG, April 14, 1919

Herr OTTO BREUER
VIENNA, VII
Kaiserstrasse

My dear Sir!

We thank you very much for your friendly lines and your mention of the essays and criticism of *Adolf Loos*. In doing so you have given us great pleasure, and we have hastened to tell Mr. *Loos* as well how happy we will be if a publication of his collected essays can come out in our edition.
Perhaps it would be best if you would begin by sending us right away by registered or insured mail the whole lot of the essays, whereby we will be able to submit our proposals concerning the arrangement and execution of the book either to you or to Mr. *Adolf Loos*.
We await your further news with eager anticipation, and for today send you our regards and repeated thanks.

Most respectfully and devotedly yours,
KURT WOLFF, Publishers

This letter has its prehistory. Originally, at the time I was working at the *neue freie presse*, I had intended to have these essays, which had appeared in this newspaper every Sunday for the duration of the Jubilee Exhibition in 1898, published as a book. The edition was to be *dekorative kunst*, published by Bruckmann in Munich, as I was the Viennese correspondent for that periodical during the first year of its publication. The publishing firm of Bruckmann, however, informed me after a year that my essays were no longer timely and sued me to return an advance of two hundred marks. The essays were put aside. Over the years many German publishers have made me offers to publish these articles. But I was against it. These essays were written for one time and in one newspaper, and I had a thousand things to think about. For didactic reasons I had to express my true opinions in sentences that years later still cause me to shudder as I read them. But even this watered-down way of writing has earned me the reputation, not with the philistines but with the "modern" artists, of attacking the *moderne* through a paradoxical way of writing. Only at the insistence of my dear students, especially the architect Otto Breuer, have I decided to consent to the publication of these essays. Among the publishers who at some point solicited the publication, either orally or in writing, I mentioned the firm of Kurt Wolff.

Mr. Breuer, who had taken great pains collecting the essays, sent them to the publisher and soon received from the publisher's reader, who is in charge of the art department, a note informing him that the publisher could only carry out the publication if I would agree to alterations and deletions of the attacks against Josef Hoffmann—who, however, was never mentioned by name.

Thereupon I took back these articles from the publishing firm of Kurt Wolff.

From the *neue Zürcher zeitung* (morning edition no. 187):
"Notice
February 5, 1921
Literary. The publishing firm of Georges Crès & Cie., Paris-Zurich, informs us by way of Paul Stefan's article of December 30 of last year that it has decided to publish the essays of Adolf Loos in its edition after, as Paul Stefan writes, no German publishing house whatsoever would dare, even on the occasion of his fiftieth birthday, to issue the collected essays of this reformer in the field of architecture and, in a broader sense, of cultural life. Adolf Loos has given his consent."

I express my gratitude to the publisher Georges Crès.

Adolf Loos
1921

The Winter Exhibition of the Austrian Museum

The Battle against the English Style (Hofrat von Scala)

Neue Freie Presse,
November 13, 1898

An Austrian who visited the great World's Fair in London in the year 1862 must have been filled with melancholy sentiments in the face of the enormous gap separating the Austrian arts and crafts from the English. Over there was the active life, new ways, struggle, disputation between parties, a searching and groping for new forms and beauty; here the torpid resignation of the Austrian handicraft workers, standstill, sluggishness. And this melancholy gave birth to a happy thought: to go to school with the English, to do exactly as the English do.

The deed followed the thought. The Austrian Museum was founded on the English model. Fortune was propitious to the new undertaking. In Eitelberger arose an inspired adherent of the English ideas, and in this way the new principles received a firm foundation and a resolute direction.

It is certainly unnecessary to state that the Viennese masses followed these aspirations mistrustfully. What, they argued, are we not Austrians? How do we come to this, to have to copy anything from the English? Proud Viennese feeling was aroused against the allegation that outside the walls of Vienna something better was being done than at home. And certainly, if one were to hear the matter from the ordinary private citizen, one could hardly refrain from commenting that the whole business only had the aim of delivering over the Austrian industries to England. Paid English agents! Then, however, a noble man of the art world defended the enterprise, and an end was put to the slander.

In spite of all the assaults on the new enterprise, the "English disease"—a favorite slogan of the earlier time—gained ground rapidly. Not to the detriment of Austrian industry. Thanks to the fact that people in Vienna were first to give the English indications of understanding, the museum on the Stubenring became the central meeting ground for the Continental arts and crafts movement. From Germany, Italy, and France came its compatriots to study the Viennese developments. Old workshops that had closed their doors to the new spirit crumbled, and new ones that had embraced it enthusiastically blossomed and quickly came to esteem. Then all at once there was a stir in Vienna. The old rubbish was thrown out; "stylish," an English word which the Viennese translated as *stilvoll*, became the watchword. And foreign countries too came and put in their orders.

But the Viennese likes to rest after his work is done, longer than is quite necessary. The Englishman does not do this. And though Vienna and London seemed for several years to march abreast (in fact, this was never the case, since London had the advantage of occupying the lead) the gap widened more and more. Germany too had relaxed a little. But when the Chicago exhibition made the Germans conscious of their distance from the rest of the civilized nations, they roused themselves and ran like lightning to catch up. By now they will already have reached their goal.

Austria, however, noticed nothing. That is, people did notice something. Namely they noticed that the arts and crafts were not going as well as they had formerly. Let's say they were downright bad. People noticed that one and the same *lusterweibchen*, which took just as much work today as twenty years ago and at that time could have been sold for five hundred florins, today, still smelling of oil paint (although the seller will swear that it comes from the estate of a female singer), could not be given away for fifty florins. People further noticed that no one came from abroad anymore to study the activities of the Viennese museum. They noticed that the Balkans, formerly a major market for Austrian arts and crafts, cold-shouldered Vienna and turned toward London. And then

132

they noticed—and this was really the most depressing part—that the imports by London furniture firms to Austria were even increasing from year to year.

What had happened? Count Latour, at that time the department head for arts and crafts in the Ministry of Education, and Herr von Scala, an intimate connoisseur of the English art situation, similar to what Eitelberger was for his time, themselves went abroad to find a clue to the cause of these depressing symptoms. And there they made the discovery that we had taken too thorough a rest. There was need for haste. The damage was enormous. Our prestige abroad had suffered profoundly. While we had formerly been the first city on the Continent for arts and crafts, we now ranked among the last. We were far, far outstripped. Here it was no longer a matter of quarreling at official levels over which style would be helpful to us, but of making use of such means as might help at all. We no longer had any choice.

Thence, the only prescription was the following: the public with the buying power in Austria and abroad must also be able to obtain in Austria that which could be bought in England and which in fact decided the buyer to go directly to England.

Everyone immediately went to work. Instead of Japanese armor and paintings of Nordic deities, as the previous direction of the museum's collection had acquired, classic English furniture and other useful objects were enrolled in the collection. The old cry that the Viennese had already been obliged to raise in 1863 against the English aspirations was again struck up. The slogan about the English disease was dusted off and again called forth out of the attic. And again it failed to prove its strength, even though the industrial and commercial opponents put forth slanderous contentions about the new museum directors of the world, even though no one shrank from asserting that Herr von Scala was bringing English-made goods into the museum for sale. But the new spirit emerged once again on the side of progress as victor of the battle. It was also in vain that the fairy tale of the "secret fund" was again served up. This fairy tale and the contention concerning the importation of English furniture had already been circulating for some time, but had never been made so blatantly public as in recent days. A formal inquiry into this "secret" fund was initiated in the provincial parliament before the end of the year by Representative Schneider, examined by the government, and found to be accurate. Certainly it was a matter of formality, for the high-minded cavaliers who out of pure friendship to the handicrafts had created and themselves administered a capital advance to the crafts workers were not supposed to be offended. But Representative Schneider was pleased enough to have initiated the inquiry.

The claim that furniture of English provenance was sold inside and outside the museum was a different matter. The English furniture that Hofrat von Scala had acquired for the museum was exhibited just like all the other objects of the museum and belonged to the museum's stock. But the books that are kept in the museum for all acquisitions show that not even one piece of that furniture was damaged, removed from the museum, or sold under the new administration. How can one actually prove this? Quite easily, in fact, because all of them are still there. Many of the deep-rooted misunderstandings would have been avoided if the true situation of things had been known earlier.

Several papers went so far as to call Hofrat von Scala a commercial traveler who travels all over buying up English furniture. It is repugnant to me to have to refute such nonsensical reproaches seriously. But it must be done. If it were so of him, he would have been representing the interests of his museum very poorly. Yet by instructing the Viennese cabinetmakers to manufacture exactly the same furniture for the millions who formerly ran over to England yearly, he renders the English a poor service.

It will be objected that I am perhaps too quick to chime in on the victory song. Perhaps Hofrat von Scala will not be able to stand firm. The end of the day is not yet at hand. However, it is not at all a matter of Herr von Scala here. For the communiqué published by the Arts and Crafts Association at the end of the battle proclaimed the ideas of Scala.

But memory serves correctly. When the Winter Exhibition opened last year, it was above all the Arts and Crafts Association which presented a united front against the new ideas. The publication of this association scoffed at the new impulses in an article that bore the significant title "The Renaissance of Pedantry." And this very summer an industrialist, one in the forefront of the struggles over the Scala tendencies, explained to the kaiser, who was viewing the exhibit of the Arts and Crafts Association, "This is a style that won't last long." No invitation was forthcoming for the exhibitor of this room, master cabinetmaker Müller, and in this way that industrialist did the honors for his absent colleagues. And now, to the general astonishment, the Arts and Crafts Association explains that it has never been an opponent of the English style, that this notion is totally erroneous. Indeed, it even refers to the work of its formerly so much maligned colleagues, about whom it writes, "Each of the hundreds of thousands of visitors to the arts and crafts section of the current Kaiser's Jubilee Exhibition in the Rotunda must and will have been convinced through his own observation that several of the most prominent and accomplished members of the Arts and Crafts Association are present"—take note, Mr. Müller, master cabinetmaker!—"who are precisely the ones that have exhibited ultramodern and, if we want to use the familiar expression, ultra-English rooms."

This declaration is truly a result about which Hofrat von Scala has reason to be proud. One has to consider that he has only done something more than a one-year administrative stint. Of course, this change in perception could not have been accomplished so noiselessly; a storm of crisis broke loose such as had not been seen within the Viennese climate of the art manufacturers for a long time. Yes, couldn't all this have been avoided?

No. It then might have taken not one year, but years. And the Austrian arts and crafts could not wait. For things are going badly for it, very badly. Of course, in those workshops that work in accordance with the Scala principles there is plenty to do day and night. New commissions cannot even be accepted. But the great majority of our arts and crafts force have difficult times to surmount. So better a few dazzling bolts of lightning and thunder than to let the whole industry wait for salvation.

Last year's Winter Exhibition had only small participation. It never regretted this. This year we are confronted with 150 firms. There was an attempt to spread the report that only small craftsmen were involved, those who "hardly could afford an instruction book. And that's the reason for the confidence! For the demonstration of unanimity!"

But how we change! The proudest names of the Austrian art industry fall upon our ears. All in all, more than 150 exhibitors. We hold our heads. Yes, but were we not told that the actions of the hofrat were directed against the so-called Austrian arts and crafts? It almost looks to us as if they have been assembled as one under his banner. Where then is the opposition?

Last year Hofrat von Scala achieved his first success through strict copies made by farseeing craftsmen. And today the Viennese arts and crafts can point to a series of new creations, all in the new spirit, the fruit of a year's work of museum administration.

Review of the Arts and Crafts, II

Die Wage, *November 26, 1898*

97 Glass vase in the style of Tiffany by the Austrian Max Ritter von Spaun. From Kunst und Kunsthandwerk, *no. 3, 1900. 98 Metal basket by Rudolf Hammel. This object was reproduced in the original article in* Die Wage.

The opening of the Winter Exhibition of the Austrian Museum has silenced with one blow the accusations raised against Hofrat von Scala. The public was able to measure the difference between the objects of the Arts and Crafts Association on exhibit and those that have issued forth under Scala's direction. And even that newspaper which formerly counted among the worst enemies of the Scala initiative carries reports about his show, while no one takes any notice at all of the Arts and Crafts Association's exhibit. Let no one say that this time the Arts and Crafts Association has found no place to show its work. In previous years, the Scala exhibition had less room, while the Arts and Crafts Association laid claim to the columned courtyard. And in spite of this the Scala exhibition received its due attention.

Indeed, the extent to which public opinion has changed can be estimated from the fact that the very paper which before the exhibition most strongly assailed the innovations of the hofrat suddenly finds that he doesn't proselytize his ideas radically enough. Still others—certainly including those who sought to construe it as detrimental to the art industry that small crafts were included in the Winter Exhibition—find that Scala does not adhere to his own program since large manufacturers also have taken part in the exhibition. To my knowledge Hofrat von Scala has never proposed such a program. On the contrary: he constantly stresses that large manufacturers and small crafts should have the same right to the house.

Still another position is deemed unjust by the Viennese arts and crafts monopolists: the inclusion of the provinces. But these comprise thirty percent of the exhibitors. They will just have to get used to it. The revolution has even been a little too radical. A year ago the museum was still a clearing house for the Arts and Crafts Association; now it belongs to the entire state.

The provinces have also given us cause for the greatest joy, especially through their copies of Tiffany glass. Ritter von Spaun of Klostermühle (in northern Bohemia) has attempted this difficult experiment and, take note, has succeeded, for the first time succeeded, although Herr von Spaun had many predecessors.

Tiffany's glass represents the standard of the art of glassmaking and glassblowing. The house of Tiffany has existed in New York for a hundred years now. With sovereign greatness it reigns today over the whole art of gold- and silverwork worldwide. In this house worked Moore, the greatest goldsmith of this century, who passed away in 1892, in the bloom of his career and young in years.[1] The elder Tiffany, one of the richest men in New York, never carried on his business in factory fashion. He operated it like a patron of the arts; Moore's work, assembled in one room as in a museum, has been piously preserved and is priceless.

The idealism of the father has been inherited by the sons. One of them, Louis C. Tiffany, himself a painter who traveled extensively around the coasts of the Mediterranean, was inspired by the magnificent glasswork of ancient Greece and ancient Rome, which today the earth is giving back to us again piece by piece. If such objects please a European, he will buy them and put them in the museum. But if an American finds them pleasing, he will build a smelting furnace, search out people capable of producing similar work, and personally undertake the venture to the best of his ability. Louis C. Tiffany dealt with things like an American. Success was not long in coming. After exemplary financial sacrifices, and with the participation of Venetian, Oriental, and Japanese workers, he succeeded in realizing the splendor of the ancient glass—not only surpassing its iridescent play of colors, but also achieving new, unanticipated effects without cutting, just by simple blowing. One can admire authentic pieces of Tiffany glass in the ground-floor room of the Austrian Museum.

There are two respects in which our homemade products still differ from the original: they lack the gleaming fires, especially in the flowing streams of color, and they lack that imperative iridescence which makes the glass so impressive. That should elicit no rebuke. It should only incite the artist to venture further in this direction. But if one reads our daily newspapers, one comes precisely to the conviction that we could rest on our accomplishments in the glass industry for another hundred years.

The glass on exhibit is also interesting with respect to its form. While the antique vases have a funnel-shaped mouth in accordance with their purpose as containers for liquid—a form which was taken over for decorative vases unthinkingly—the exhibited forms show us clearly and unmistakably that they are containers for holding long-stemmed flowers. The crocus-shaped mouth in this way constitutes a support, whereas the funnel-shaped opening could easily cause the glass to fall over.

The architect Hammel has distinguished himself throughout the exhibition. Two interiors originate from him, and countless individual objects give evidence of his imagination. Hammel's work does not make us shout with joy, but it works on us agreeably. It is agreeable, that is, because it modestly seeks to subordinate itself to a technique and because it is not so precious as the work of his modern colleagues at the drawing board. He has an ease and naiveté about his work that remind us of the Americans.

The fundamental principle of the Scala vision emerges sharply in the Winter Exhibition: either imitate exactly, or create something new. There is no third way. Certainly such exact copies strike us as something strange. But they have the advantage that they always maintain their beauty, whereas we become weary of those misbegotten "stylish" pieces of furniture after a short time. The German Renaissance did not go out of fashion, only its botched-up copies. Old towns, old castles, old town halls still affect us today with the same power as twenty years ago. But we flee with horror from the "stylish" dining room.

The Secession also has a whole room devoted to the applied arts. Gurschner's bronzes, especially the charming door knocker, have captivated the Viennese. They are pleasing and would surely also be significant if Gurschner had not relied so much on Vallgren.[2] Zelezny's witch, a mask made out of pearwood with glass eyes, found a fancier on the very first day. The embroideries called "The Three Fates" by Hélène de Rudder of Brussels prove to be extraordinary. Both of the blotters by Adolf Böhm, of inlaid multicolored leather, and—last but not least—the furniture by Friedrich Otto Schmidt are masterpieces, each in its own way.

99 Bronze door knocker, G. Gurschner. From Ver Sacrum, *no. 1, 1898.*

Appendix essays translated by Joan Ockman

The following notes are provided by the editor. Author's footnotes, with those added in 1931 so noted, appear in the margin contiguous to the reference.

Foreword
1. German common nouns are conventionally capitalized.
2. Grimm (1785-1863) was a German philologist who, in addition to collecting *Grimm's Fairy Tales* with his brother Wilhelm, wrote major works on German grammar and inaugurated the *Grimm Dictionary* of the German language. In the *Grimm Dictionary*, all initials of non-proper nouns are in the lower case, including even the initials of the first words of sentences (Loos does not follow the latter procedure here).
3. A German typeface similar to English Gothic or black letter.

The Leather Goods and Gold- and Silversmith Trade
1. In 1893. Loos lived in America from 1893 to 1896, visiting the World's Columbian Exposition in Chicago in 1893.
2. The location of the Austrian Museum for Art and Industry. The role of this museum under the direction of Anton von Scala is discussed at length in later essays.

Men's Fashion
1. "In November 1786 a pamphlet called 'Project for a New Dress Code Regulation to Be Observed This Coming Year in Vienna' was published. The anonymous author decried the fact that anyone could dress as luxuriously as his means allowed and lamented the outrages that could result: a member of the aristocracy could be addressed by a craftsman with the familiar 'thou'—or even less respectfully—simply because his coat was of simple cloth, or, as happened not infrequently, hairdressers and servants could be greeted politely in stores and other public places and even given preferential treatment just because they were dressed in the latest fashions. The unknown writer proposed subtle regulations of dress that would make it possible to recognize a man's trade or quality of birth by the way he dressed; these rules would be enforced by a 'dress police.' Despite the author's emotional tone, one important fact is clear: the privilege of the upper classes to distinguish themselves by their dress had been abandoned in Vienna well before the time of the French Revolution." Dora Heinz, "Viennese Men's Fashion," in *The Imperial Style: Fashions of the Hapsburg Era* (New York: The Metropolitan Museum of Art, 1980), p. 101.
2. Friedrich Theodor Vischer (1807-1887),

German aesthetic philosopher and critic; his chief work was the *Aesthetik*.
3. Karl Wilhelm Diefenbach (1851-1913), German painter and stylish apostle of a "natural" way of life.
4. Gustav Jäger [Jaeger] (1832-1916), German zoologist who directed the Vienna Zoo from 1867 to 1884. In 1880 he wrote his book *My System* introducing *Jägerhemden* or hygienic woolen underwear, which gained him an international following.

The New Style and the Bronze Industry
1. The *Exposition Universelle* of 1899-1900. Preparations for this international exhibition in Paris began abroad in 1895.
2. Anton von Scala, director of the Austrian Museum for Art and Industry. His title *hofrat* is that given to an Austrian civil servant of high rank.
3. Franz von Lenbach (1836-1904), German portrait painter who worked in a style derivative of Titian and Rembrandt.

Interiors: A Prelude
1. The Makart bouquet is an elaborate arrangement of dried flowers, leaves, and fruits which was especially popular as an interior decoration in Vienna in the 1880s. It was invented by Hans Makart (1840-1884), who was the epitome of nineteenth-century academic art. The most renowned painter in Vienna during the second half of the century as well as the greatest illusionist and decorator, his ornate style with its evocations of Rococo and legendary splendor is identified with the heyday of the Ringstrasse.
2. Josef Pletschnik [Plečnik] (1872-1957), architect of the Vienna Secession and member of the Otto Wagner School. Among his most notable works are the Zacherl House (1903-1905) and the Heilig-Geist Church (1910-1912).

Interiors in the Rotunda
1. *Dekorationsdivan.*
2. Wilhelm Exner (1840-1931), an engineer and technologist from a well-to-do railroad family. He served as a highly effective director of the Museum of Technological Trades (*Technologische Gewerbemuseum*) from 1879 to 1904.

Furniture for Sitting
1. Wagner's full title, *K. K. Oberbaurat*, means "Royal and Imperial Chief Building Councillor"; he was given it in 1894.

Glass and Clay
1. A city in Bohemia known at the time for its imitations of Tiffany glass. The factory of Graf von Harrach was located there.

The Luxury Vehicle
1. *Reservevorlegebalken.*
2. *Ortscheiten.* The crossbars that support the springs.
3. *Riemennetz.*

Plumbers
1. *Die englische Krankheit.* A play on the German expression for rickets.
2. Johann Christoph Gottsched (1700-1766), German literary critic, philosopher, and disciple of the French Enlightenment. He exerted a powerful effect upon eighteenth-century German letters and was the primary exponent of epigonal aesthetic theory in literature, advocating imitation of the great French classical dramatists and poets as models for German literature.
3. Ludwig I of Bavaria (1786-1868), king of Bavaria from 1825 to 1848. He was chiefly responsible for transforming Munich into one of the handsomest capitals of Europe and making it a center of the arts; his reign, liberal at first, became reactionary, and he was forced to abdicate during the Revolution of 1848 in favor of his son Maximilian II.
4. *Die Fliegende Blätter,* a German satirical magazine published in Munich from 1844 to 1944.
5. The Martinswand is a steep and rocky wall in the Tyrolean Alps. According to legend Emperor Maximilian I was rescued by an angel from a cavern there.
6. The Fuggers were a German family of merchants and bankers that rose from poor weavers to become one of the richest houses in Europe in the fifteenth and sixteenth centuries. Their palatial house in Augsburg was famous for its artistic and opulent decor, and included two so-called *Badezimmer,* whose walls were lavishly painted with grotesques in the Italianate style by Antonio Ponzano, 1570-1572.
7. *Junges Deutschland* was a group of radical writers and poets in Germany in the 1830s. Heinrich Laube (1806-1884) was a prominent member of the group. *Die Krieger* [The Warrior] is the title of the second book of his three-volume novel *Das Junge Europa;* it appeared in 1837.
8. Vincenz Priessnitz (1799-1852), a Silesian peasant without formal training in medicine who gained international fame at his clinic in Graefenberg, where he prescribed water cures, cleanliness, exercise, and rustic living.
9. Sebastian Kniepp (1821-1897), a humanitarian priest and healer who worked in the village of Woerishofen in Bavaria. After being cured of a serious illness by water, he devoted himself to promoting a program of hydrotherapy which included various kinds of baths and ablutions, exposure to cold water, and prescribed water drinking, as well as healthful dietary habits and the medicinal use of herbs. In 1890 he published his book *Meine Wassercur* [My Water Cure] which appealed to a wide audience; cures, spas, and other products bearing his name were sold internationally and were especially popular in the United States.

Footwear
1. Perhaps Rigó Tanya, a town in present-day Czechoslovakia between Vienna and Budapest, at that time part of Austria.
2. Heinrich Clauren, pseudonym of Karl Gottlieb Samuel Heun (1771-1854), writer of sentimental love stories.

Shoemakers
1. A region in the northeastern part of present-day Rumania and the western Ukraine; it was a provincial district of Austria from 1775 to 1918.
2. Hans Sachs (1494-1576), German poet of the Nuremberg school and a shoemaker and guild master; he is the principal character in Richard Wagner's opera *Die Meistersinger.* Jakob Böhme [Boehm] (1575-1624), the religious mystic and philosopher, started out as a cobbler in the German town of Görlitz.
3. *Leaves of Grass and Selected Prose* (New York: Random House, 1950), p. 184.

The Principle of Cladding
1. *Bekleidung.* "*Bekleidung* signifies the external covering of the building materials by other materials, either for technical reasons—for example, weatherproofing—or aesthetic ones. . . . The problem of so-called correctness of materials [*Materialgerechtheit*] is closely related to the question of *Bekleidung*" (*Wasmuths Lexikon der Baukunst* [Leipzig, 1932]). The root *Kleidung* means "clothing."
2. Besides its general meaning of "covering" or "blanket," and its architectural meaning of "ceiling" or "roof," in anatomy *Decke* signifies the skin or coat of an animal.
3. Friedrich Schmidt (1825-1891), Theophil Hansen (1813-1891), and Heinrich von Ferstel (1828-1883) were three of the chief architects of the Vienna Ringstrasse, most of which was built from 1861 to 1865 and from 1868 to 1873. Vienna University, in the Italian Renaissance style, was built by Ferstel from 1873 to 1884. Ferstel also designed and built the Austrian Museum for Art and Industry; it was completed in 1871.
4. Tiles made out of crushed pieces of pottery.

Underclothes
1. A cowboy of the Hungarian plains.
2. Present-day Plovdiv, a city in south central Bulgaria.

Furniture
1. A preparation of green varnish with gold powder, introduced by the Martin family in France under Louis XV and used as a finish for furniture.

Furniture of the Year 1898
1. The Rochlitz Secession was a movement at the beginning of the sixteenth century in which the brotherhood of masons (*Bauhütte*) of the Saxon city of Rochlitz declared its independence from the powerful Strassburg brotherhood and attempted to set up its own *Bauhütte*.
2. Jamnitzer (1508-1585) was a Viennese goldsmith and engraver who worked in Nuremberg; a leading craftsman of his day, he executed precious work for the royal court, the nobility, and the church. His refined craftsmanship reflects the influence of Italian Mannerism.

Printers
1. Jules Chéret (1836-1932), French lithographer and decorative painter. As one of the originators of the Art Nouveau poster, he improved upon color lithography techniques and produced vivid, direct designs characterized by bold coloration and outline drawing, abolition of unnecessary details, and a concise text; his posters of dancing girls were extremely popular.
2. Will Bradley (1868-1962), printer, type designer, artist, and illustrator. Strongly influenced by the English Arts and Crafts Movement, he was one of the major proponents of the Art Nouveau style in America. His typographic work of the 1890s using the Caslon typeface was based on the work of the colonial printers and was responsible "for converting printers of the United States to a style which is at once sane, pleasing, and artistic" (*The American Handbook of Printing*, 3d ed. [New York, 1913]).

School Exhibition of the School of Applied Arts
1. Sir Lawrence Alma-Tadema (1836-1912), English painter who worked in Belgium and England; his academic and meticulous paintings of intimate classical subjects enjoyed great popularity.

The Christmas Exhibition at the Austrian Museum
1. Rudolf von Eitelberger (1817-1885), an art historian and strong advocate of the applied arts who was largely responsible for the establishment of the Austrian Museum for Art and Industry in 1863, becoming its first director. He also founded the associated *Kunstgewerbeschule*, the School of Applied Arts, in 1868. The museum and school were based on his conception of a state-supported handicraft industry brought into the modern industrial age.
2. Daniel Nikolaus Chodowiecki (1726-1801), a German engraver and the most popular illustrator of his day.
3. The so-called *Gschnaszimmer*, an elaborately decorated salon found in the aristocratic palaces on the Ringstrasse, takes its name from the *Gschnasfest*, a carnival-ball celebrated in Austria at Shrovetide just before Ash Wednesday. The first *Gschnasfest* was held in Vienna in 1870, with numerous Viennese artists collaborating on the large set decorations.

Potemkin City
1. Grigori Aleksandrovich Potemkin (1739-1791), Russian field marshal and favorite of Catherine II, is supposed to have erected sham villages in the newly annexed Crimea in order to impress the empress with the region's prosperity during her tour there in 1787.

Ladies' Fashion
1. These paragraphs of the Austrian Penal Act concern "rape, debauchment, and other cases involving serious lewdness."
2. Leopold Ritter von Sacher-Masoch (1835-1895) was an Austrian novelist; his stories depict an attitude by which pleasure is derived from sexual or psychological pain, hence "masochism." Catulle Mendès (1841-1909) and Paul Armand Silvestre (1862-1915) were among the principal members of the Parnassian school of French poets who practiced a doctrine of art for art's sake derived from Baudelaire and Théophile Gautier. Their writing, a reaction to what they perceived as Romantic looseness, centers on exotic and classical subjects and is characterized by its exact craftsmanship, rigidity of form, and emotional detachment.
3. In his "Eulogy for Peter Altenberg" of 1919, Loos writes that the eccentric poet "always had a small handout for abused children about whom he came to hear in the newspapers. 'Peter Altenberg—10 crowns.' It was a standing notice in the bulletin of the Children's Protection and Rescue Society."
4. The "Five Sisters Barrison" were a family of young American dancers who were popular on the stage in Europe in the 1890s; their variations on the cancan brought the Jugendstil into dance.

Review of the Arts and Crafts

1. Liberty's, established in 1875 by Sir Arthur Lasenby Liberty on Regent Street, by the 1890s specialized in fabrics, wallpapers, porcelain, and metalware, much of it inspired by Oriental motifs. The store was a meeting place for the leading figures of both the Aesthetic and the Arts and Crafts Movements.

2. The Maison de l'Art Nouveau on the Rue de Provence in Paris, established in 1895 by the influential German art dealer Samuel Bing, was a showcase for international developments in the Art Nouveau style. The shop featured Tiffany glassware; furniture, ceramics, and jewelry from Bing's own workshops; and products of fine and applied art by nearly every other major artist of the movement.

3. Klinger (1857-1920) was a German painter, sculptor, and etcher whose religious-allegorical paintings and portrait sculptures were featured in exhibitions at the Vienna Secession.

4. A mountain pass on the boundary between Lower Austria and Styria, fifty miles southwest of Vienna.

5. "Les Bijoux aux Salons de 1898," *Art et Décoration*, June [*sic*] 1898, pp. 169-178.

English Schools in the Austrian Museum

1. Two well-known Viennese firms of the day; Förster specialized in imported luxury leather goods, Würzl in leather goods of all kinds.

2. Hacker (1858-1919) was a popular painter of society portraits; he also produced paintings of genre and historical scenes in the Romantic manner.

3. Brown (1851-1941) was a landscape and genre painter, watercolorist, and, Loos's statement to the contrary, a distinguished teacher at the Westminster School of Art from 1892 to 1918.

The Scala Theater in Vienna

1. The title of this article probably plays on the name of Anton von Scala and the great Milanese opera house. The form of the article may have been suggested to Loos by the place where it was published: *Die Wage* [The Scales], a weekly newspaper published and edited by Rudolf Lothar with regular contributions from Karl Kraus, was devoted primarily to criticism of the theater and politics.

2. What is permitted to cows/To Jove is not allowed.

3. Maple and Henry were two large commercial furniture firms in London.

My Appearance on Stage with Melba

1. Nellie Melba (1861-1931), the most celebrated soprano of the day. Born in Melbourne, Australia, the source of her stage name, she sang at the Metropolitan Opera in New York during various seasons from 1893 to 1910.

2. [The New York Standard-Bearer]. This and the two newspapers mentioned subsequently, the *New-Yorker Staatszeitung* [The New York City Paper] and the *Morgenposaune* [The Morning Herald], were probably German-American newspapers published for the Germanic or German-Jewish community around New York. We have been unable to find any record in papers with these or similar titles of the series of events that Loos recounts here. The performance of *Carmen* to which he refers took place on February 3, 1896 (not 1895).

The Poor Little Rich Man

1. A piece of music composed by Johann Strauss the Elder in 1848 in honor of Field Marshal Radetzky, the most popular Austrian commander of his time.

Review of the Arts and Crafts, II

1. Edward C. Moore (born 1827), presiding genius of Tiffany's silverware business until his death in 1891 [*sic*]. Not a goldsmith but a silversmith, Moore's work was strongly inspired by Oriental art and was considered to have ushered in a "new style" in silverwork.

2. Victor Vallgren, metal sculptor working in Paris at the time. Numerous objects by him in the Art Nouveau style, most of them out of bronze, appear in the first catalogue of Samuel Bing's Maison de l'Art Nouveau.

Figure Credits

Jacket, 1 © COSMOPRESS, Geneva, and ADAGP, Paris, 1982.

2, 59 Courtesy Albertina Museum, Vienna.

3-4 From *Beautiful Scenes of the White City: A Portfolio of Original Copper-Plate Half-Tones of the World's Fair—Farewell Edition* (Chicago: Land & Lee Publishers, 1894).

5, 20, 73 From *Das Interieur: Wiener Monatshefte für Angewandte Kunst II* (Vienna, 1901).

6 From *Das Andere: Ein Blatt zur Einfuehrung Abendlaendischer Kultur in Oesterreich: Geschrieben von Adolf Loos*, no. 2 (Vienna, 1903).

7, 61 From *Das Andere*, no. 1 (Vienna, 1903).

8 From *Simplicissimus: Illustrierte Wochenschrift*, vol. 7 (Munich, 1902).

9 From J. P. Thornton, *The Sectional System of Gentlemen's Garment Cutting, Comprising Coats, Vests, Breeches, and Trousers* (London: Minister & Co., 1887).

10 From *Innen Dekoration*, vol. 11 (Vienna, September 1900).

11 From *Innen Dekoration*, vol. 10 (Vienna, October 1899)

12, 46, 65-66 From *Das Interieur I* (Vienna, 1900).

13 Photograph courtesy Hermann Czech.

14 From Fred Hennings, *Ringstrassen Symphonie* (Vienna: Verlag Herold, 1963-64).

15 From *Blätter für Kunstgewerbe: Organ des Wiener Kunstgewerbe-Vereins*, vol. 7 (Vienna, 1898).

16, 19, 54, 99 From *Ver Sacrum: Organ der Vereinigung Bildender Künstler Oesterreichs*, no. 1 (Vienna, October 1898).

17-18 From Otto Wagner, *Einige Skizzen, Projekte, und Ausgefuhrte Bauwerke von Otto Wagner*, vol. 2 (Vienna: A. Schroll, 1897).

21 From *Kunst und Handwerk*, vol. 51 (Munich, 1900).

22 From *Das Interieur III* (Vienna, 1902).

23 Courtesy Lord & Taylor, New York.

24 From Walter A. Dyer and Esther Stevens Fraser, *The Rocking Chair: An American Institution* (New York and London: The Century Co., 1928).

25 Courtesy Joseph Hummel.

26-27 From Gottfried Semper, *Der Stil in den Technischen und Tektonischen Künsten, oder Praktische Aesthetik* (Munich: Friedrich Bruckmann's Verlag, 1879).

28, 69, 74-78, 93 From *Kunst und Kunsthandwerk: Monatsschrift des K. K. Österr. Museums fuer Kunst und Industrie*, no. 1 (Vienna: Artaria & Co., 1898).

29, 92, 94-96 From *Kunst und Kunsthandwerk*, no. 2 (Vienna, 1899).

30 From *The Carriage Monthly*, vol. 32 (Philadelphia, October 1896).

31 From Max Reinsch, *100 Moderne Wagen* (Ravensberg: Verlag von Otto Maier, 1896).

32 From *Zeitschrift für Architekten- und Ingenieurwesen zu Hannover* (Hanover: Schmorl & Von Seefeld, 1873).

33-37 From Franz Merklein, *Praktisches Handbuch für den Gesammten Wagenbau*, Atlas (Vienna, Pest, and Leipzig: A. Hartleben's Verlag, 1896).

38 From *The Plumbers' Journal: Gas, Steam, and Hot Water Fitters' Review*, vol. 27 (Chicago, 1900).

39 From William Paul Gerhard, *Entwasserungs-Anlagen Amerikanischer Gebäude. Fortschritte auf dem Gebiete der Architektur: Erganzungshefte zum Handbuch der Architektur*, no. 10 (Stuttgart: A. Bergsträsser, 1897).

40 From *Neue Freie Presse* (Vienna, August 28, 1898).

41 From *Neue Freie Presse* (Vienna, September 25, 1898).

42 From *Wiener Bauindustrie-Zeitung*, no. 32 (Vienna, 1902).

43 From Siegfried Giedion, *Mechanization Takes Command* (New York: Oxford University Press, 1955).

44, 67 From *Das Interieur IV* (Vienna, 1903).

45 From Philo vom Walde [Johannes Reinelt], *Vincenz Priessnitz: Sein Leben und Sein Wirken* (Berlin: W. Möller, 1898). Courtesy Yale University Medical School Library.

47-49 From Carl Bortfeldt, *Die Hutmacherkunst: Ein Handbuch für den Klein- und Grossbetrieb* (Leipzig: Verlag B. F. Voight, 1902).

50 From *Europäische Moden-Zeitung für Herren-Garderobe*, no. 9 (1865). Reprinted in *Zum Funfundzwanzigjährigen Bestehen der "Modenwelt" 1865-1890* (Leipzig: O. Dürr, 1890).

51 From *The Tailor and Cutter* (London, 1902). Reprinted from Phillis Cunningham and Alan Mansfield, *English Costume for Sports and Outdoor Recreation* (London: Adam and Charles Black, 1969).

52, 83-84, 86-88 From Max von Boehn, *Bekleidungskunst und Mode* (Munich: Delphin-Verlag, 1918).

53 From *The Illustrated News* (London, March 6, 1897). Reprinted from Cunningham and Mansfield, *English Costume for Sports and Outdoor Recreation.*

55-56 From *The London Shoe Company Catalogue* (London, c. 1890).

57 From Bernhard Rodegast, *Die Fusskleidungskunst* (Leipzig, B. F. Voight, 1905).

58 From *Der Bazar: Illustrierte Damen Zeitung* (Berlin, December 14, 1891).

60 From Paul Kortz, *Wien am Anfang des Jahrhunderts. Ein Führer in Technischer und Künstlerischer Richtung, hrsg. vom Osterreichisches Ingenieur- und Architekten-Verein* (Vienna: Gerlach & Wiedling, 1905-6).

62, 63 From *Illustrated Catalogue and Price List of Doctor Jaeger's Sanitary Woolen System Company* (New York, 1887).

64 From Hans Gunther Sperlich, *Versuch über Joseph Maria Olbrich* (Darmstadt: J. von Liebig, 1965).

68 From *The American Handbook of Printing* (New York: Oswald Publishing Company, 3d ed., 1913).

70-72 From *Die Wiener Werkstätte 1903-1928: Modernes Kunstgewerbe und Sein Weg* (Vienna: Krystall Verlag, 1929).

79 From *Figaro: Wiener Luft*, no. 27 (Vienna, 1883). Reprinted from Renate Wagner-Rieger, ed., *Die Wiener Ringstrasse—Bild einer Epoche* (Vienna: H. Böhlaus, 1969).

80-81 From *Die Wiener Ringstrasse in Ihrer Vollendung und der Franz Josefs-Quai* (Vienna: Manz, 1873).

82 From *Simplicissimus: Illustrierte Wochenschrift*, vol. 9 (Munich, 1904).

85 From *Wiener-Chic: Mode Journal* (Vienna, 1901).

89 From *Die Wage* (Vienna, October 1, 1898).

90 From *Art et Décoration*, no. 4 (Paris, June 1898).

91 From *Kunst und Kunsthandwerk*, no. 4 (Vienna, 1901).

97 From *Kunst und Kunsthandwerk*, no. 3 (Vienna, 1900).

98 From *Die Wage* (Vienna, November 26, 1898).